PLAINS FOLK

PLAINS FOLK

A Commonplace of the Great Plains

BY JIM HOY AND TOM ISERN

Drawings by Don Johnson

UNIVERSITY OF OKLAHOMA PRESS

NORMAN AND LONDON

BY JIM HOY
(with John Somer) *The Language Experience* (New York, 1974)
The Cattle Guard: Its History and Lore (Lawrence, 1982)
Cassoday, Cow Capital of Kansas (El Dorado, Kansas, 1984)
(with Tom Isern) *Plains Folk: A Commonplace of the Great Plains* (Norman, 1987)

BY TOM ISERN
Custom Combining on the Great Plains: A History (Norman, 1982)
(with Jim Hoy) *Plains Folk: A Commonplace of the Great Plains* (Norman, 1987)

Library of Congress Cataloging-in-Publication Data

Hoy, Jim, 1939–
  Plains folk.

  Includes index.
  1. Great Plains—Social life and customs.
  2. Farm life—Great Plains. 3. Folklore—
  Great Plains. I. Isern, Thomas D. (Thomas
  Dean), 1952–   . II. Title.
  F595.2.H68 1987   978   87–5082
  ISBN 0–8061–2064–9

The paper in this book meets the guidelines for permanence and durability of the Committee on Production Guidelines for Book Longevity of the Council on Library Resources, Inc.

Contents

The Great Plains

Great Plains Boundary · · · · ·

THE GREAT PLAINS of North America, one of four great grasslands of the world, encompass large portions of ten of the United States and three of the Canadian provinces. Stretching from the south Texas brush country to the Canadian parklands, from the Rocky Mountains to the tallgrass prairies of the Missouri-Mississippi basin, the Great Plains comprise 561 million acres, 12 percent of the land area of North America north of Mexico. The American section of the region is host to 37 million cattle and 58 million acres of wheat, 32 percent and 68 percent respectively of the national totals. North of forty-nine degrees, Saskatchewan alone produces 66 percent of the wheat in Canada. All this wheat and all these cattle coexist with some 15 million people, just 6 percent of the total population of the two countries.

Although the bedrock of the Great Plains economy is agriculture, not all the people who live here are farmers or ranchers—far from it. Only 6.8 percent of the people employed in our home state of Kansas, for instance, are farm or ranch operators or employees. The towns and cities of the Great Plains have their merchants, mechanics, police officers, physicians, dentists, lawyers, factory workers, civil servants, bankers, teachers, insurance agents, and stock brokers—the same mix found in communities across either nation. The countryside contains (in addition to farmers, ranchers, and cowboys) oil-field workers, railroaders, construction workers, soldiers, and pipeliners—again the same kinds of jobs that can be found in almost any other part of the United States or Canada. The Great Plains also contain many different ethnic and religious groups amid the dominant Anglo-Protestant culture—among others, Germans (from Germany, Russia, Switzerland, and other previous residences), French, Scandinavians, Mexicans, Italians, Métis, and Indians; Lutherans, Roman Catholics, Hutterites, Baptists, Methodists, Mennonites, Amish, Russian Orthodox, and (with the recent influx of Indochinese) Buddhists. Although sometimes found in heavier concentrations in the Great Plains, none of these groups is unique to the region.

Mixed in the Golden Bowl of the North American plains, however, these ordinary-seeming ingredients have produced a culture, a character that is distinct, in some respects unique. While plains folk share the rural and small-town culture of other predominantly agricultural areas, they have, like people in other distinct geographical regions of the world, reshaped common songs, stories, customs, attitudes, and tools to the special needs and conditions of the plains. Cattle-raising agriculturists and nomadic hunters, for instance, were to be found in many parts of the continent and the globe in the latter half of the nineteenth century, but it was the Great Plains that gave the world two of its most evocative images—the cowboy and the Indian. The plains have also given the world more prosaic gifts, such as the flyswatter and the hamburger (both invented by Kansans in the early twentieth century).

One task that we decline is to define the exact areal boundaries of the region about which we write. Let the geographers haggle over that. For convenience we include among our illustrations a map of the plains drafted by one of our geographer colleagues, but more important to our thoughts than lines on a map,are the essential characteristics of the region—the things that tell what the plains are, not just where they are. The greatest of Great Plains historians, Walter Prescott Webb, characterized the plains truly (if inexactly) as flat, treeless, and semiarid. Typically, this characterization carries negative connotations: most thought about the plains begins with a catalog of what they lack, namely, mountains, trees, and rainfall. To restate these facts in a positive manner—to say that the plains have expansive vistas, lush grasslands, and blue skies—does not change them in substance.

We can no more ignore the effects of these environmental traits than we can alter them. While we are not among the determinists who say that environment dictates culture, we do recognize that it at least constrains and often shapes culture. We cannot attribute all human phenomena to environment, but as scholars of a region we can relate all things in that region to environment, even if the relationship is one of antagonism or insulation. That, after all, is what defines regional thought.

The chapters in this book represent some of our attempts to explore the culture of the plains, to seek out its uniquenesses as well as its commonalities with other folk regions. Just as the Great Plains were the last major land area of the continent to be settled (the Oklahoma land runs of 1889 and 1893 marked, for Frederick Jackson Turner as well as for the land-hungry homesteaders, the closing of the frontier), so their distinctive folk culture has been little examined, especially in comparison to other regional cultures such as the Appalachian or the Ozark or the French-Canadian. We hope, in this collection, to communicate the sense of region, to show the bonds of community, of shared customs and traditions that exist among all plains dwellers, from Canadian, Texas, to the Canadian Prairie Provinces.

Although most people think of the Great Plains in east-west terms (especially while driving across on an interstate highway), the primary orientation of the plains is north-south. The same directions, in the words of Ogallala Sioux holy man Black Elk, that mark the good red road that was followed by the bison and the waterfowl in their migrations and by the Indians themselves during the time of their freedom. The same directions followed by Texas cattlemen who shipped their steers from Kansas and Nebraska railheads, then trailed breeding herds north to Wyoming, Montana, and Alberta in the later nineteenth century. The same directions followed today by custom combiners as they follow the wheat harvest from Oklahoma through the Dakotas and on into Saskatchewan. The plains may run east and west, but they stretch north and south, carrying with them an outlook on life that reflects an integrity of region.

It is this integrity of region that we have been writing about for over two years in our newspaper column, *Plains*

Folk. We bring to our writing both academic and personal credentials. Isern is a German name, and Tom was reared on a wheat farm near Ellinwood, in central Kansas, where his great-grandparents immigrated a century ago from Ohio and Missouri. Hoy bears the Scotch-Irish name of his great-grandfather, who moved from Ohio to the pasture country of the Kansas Flint Hills near present-day Cassoday shortly after the Civil War. Both are members of the Great Plains Studies faculty of Emporia (Kansas) State University, where Isern is a historian and Hoy a professor of English. Our personal interest in the Great Plains is thus innate, our professional interest acquired, but we hope neither interest provincial. Instead, we believe that the examination of the culture of the plains region, begun by such people as Walter P. Webb, J. Frank Dobie, and James C. Malin, is a valid pursuit, one we are attempting to further. We also believe that deeper thought about the cultural experience of the plains will enrich the lives and enhance the self-image of our fellow plains dwellers.

In looking over *Plains Folk* columns of the past few years, reworking them for this anthology, we have paused for a moment of introspection. We are natives of the plains who have lived in the region, have taken university education ("higher education," they call it, although we both went to places of lower altitude to get it), and have come to teach and research for an institution that emphasizes the study of the plains. We often write from personal experience, and our experiences progress from agricultural boyhoods to current scholarly research. The line between these is blurred, and we spend little effort attempting to focus it. Neither did Webb, or Dobie, or John Lomax, the country's foremost collector of folk songs.

As university professors we enjoy an enviable situation: it is our business to poke into the culture of the Great Plains, to explore our own roots. *Plains Folk* is the trail we leave. A reader has suggested that *Plains Folk* is our scrapbook. We think, rather, that it is more a commonplace book (hence our subtitle). Not many people keep commonplace books today, but nineteenth-century Americans did, including Americans on the frontier of the central plains. They were registers of all high thoughts, well-turned phrases, and memorable images that occurred to the writers and seemed worthy of recording for future reference. Samuel Tappan, a fiery free-soiler in Bleeding Kansas's territorial struggle over slavery, kept a commonplace book, and he continued recording thoughts in it while he joined in the Pikes Peak gold rush, fought for the Union in New Mexico, and returned to fight Confederate Missourians in Kansas. If he could keep up his literary efforts in the saddle, then surely we can do likewise in our offices.

One more caveat seems in order. We say here that our subject is the Great Plains of North America, but our writing often seems more local than that. Much of it treats personal experiences that happened in particular places, and because we both hail from Kansas, that state gets quite a bit of attention. We do not claim to give equal attention to all states, provinces, or subregions of the international plains. Still, although it is difficult to substantiate, we believe that because the various parts of the plains have certain environmental and cultural similarities—the integrity of region that we mentioned earlier—local experiences generally parallel and exemplify regional experiences.

We would like to express our gratitude to the many people who help us in our exploration of plains history and lore. Prominent among these is Patrick O'Brien, Professor of History in Emporia State University and originator and director of its Center for Great Plains Studies (without which our work would not have begun). Librarians are a necessity of scholarly life, and we owe special recognition to Steve Hanschu, Sue Hatfield, Nannette Martin, and Barb Robins, of the William Allen White Library, at Emporia State. Editors who have expressed their confidence in our work in a most concrete way—by publishing our column—include Danny Andrews and Doug McDonough, of the *Plainview* (Texas) *Daily Herald;* Keith Blackledge, of the *North Platte* (Nebraska) *Telegraph;* David Clymer, of the *El*

Dorado (Kansas) *Times;* Robert Estes and Ed Kessinger, of the *Ellinwood* (Kansas) *Leader;* Earl Loganbill, of the Beloit, Kansas, *Solomon Valley Post;* Ken Maher, of the *Mandan* (North Dakota) *Finder;* Don McNeal, of the *Council Grove* (Kansas) *Republican;* Bill Meyer, of the Marion, Kansas, *Marion County Record;* and Martin Puntney, of the *Arkansas City* (Kansas) *Traveler.* Most of all we want to thank our readers and other residents of the plains who lend us their recollections, their criticism, and their support. They are the Plains Folk.

Emporia, Kansas

JIM HOY
TOM ISERN

Part One

LEGENDS AND LORE

I SUPPOSE it is possible for some people to spend their entire lives on the Great Plains without ever encountering a rattlesnake, but I've never heard anyone admit to it. It's much more common for them to have all sorts of snake stories, exaggerated or otherwise.

As a result of increased human population in the Great Plains and the accompanying destruction of habitat, along with the highly publicized rattlesnake roundups in the southern plains, rattlers no longer pose the danger they did in pioneer days. Still, some of the pioneer superstitions and lore can be found in present-day attitudes.

I remember as a child, for example, learning as "fact" that you had to be especially wary of a site where you had killed a rattlesnake, for its mate was sure to return to look for it. I also learned that a rattler would not crawl over a rope, so when some friends and I would ride into the Flint Hills for an overnight campout, we would circle lariats around our blankets. Later I was told that the rope should have been made of horsehair to be effective, but we thought our sisal would work—it seemed stickery enough.

Another rattlesnake superstition was that the rattle off a snake you had killed, placed in a sweatband, would ward off headaches. Some people put the rattles in their hatbands, but I always thought that was more for show than for headache protection.

A superstition involving all snakes was that if you turned a freshly killed snake belly up, rain would fall within three days. Rattlers, because of the awe they inspired, were supposed to bring big rains, not just the showers you could expect from a mere garter snake.

I remember one cattle-driving lane that always seemed to have rattlesnakes. We would kill them, either by throwing rocks at them or by putting a hairpin loop in a lariat rope and hitting them with it. A sharp blow from the rope caused a broken back, and the snake's head could then be

4 LEGENDS AND LORES

crushed with a boot heel and the rattles pulled off. (I have a feeling, by the way, that 95 percent of all rattlers killed have their rattles removed as souvenirs.)

Recently I have been warned against killing a rattlesnake with a lariat because the snake's fangs might become broken off in it and one could get poisoned while coiling the rope. I haven't known this to happen, but it seems plausible enough. And that reminds me of a contemporary folk legend—the poisoned boots.

I first heard this story nearly a quarter century ago when I was visiting Raymond and Melba Prewitt just south of Cassoday, Kansas. Among other things that evening, Raymond mentioned hearing about some man, he couldn't remember just who, south of Rosalia who had married a woman recently widowed when her first husband had been struck in the foot by a rattlesnake. By chance both men had the same-size feet, and husband No. 2 started wearing various pairs of No. 1's boots. When No. 2 died, for no apparent reason, an autopsy showed rattlesnake venom as the cause. The broken-off fangs had, quite literally, struck again.

Raymond had told the story in all good faith, and as I later learned in a folklore class (where variations of this very same story were told), this is one of the hallmarks of a contemporary legend. Herpetologists have told me that a fang in a boot might cause infection but would not carry venom. But while folk belief might not square with scientific knowledge, it is totally accurate as far as morality and socially acceptable behavior go: a widow should not remarry too quickly, and husband No. 2 should certainly not attempt to take over too completely. The first husband's boots, after all, can never rightly be filled by anyone else.—*JH*

2.   *La Llorona*

FROM native American Indians to refugees recently arrived from Indochina, every national group that inhabits the

Great Plains brought with it a shared treasure of folktales—traditional stories passed on by word of mouth. For instance, unknown to most Anglo-Americans, there still exists in most substantial railroad towns of the region a rich heritage of Mexican stories imported in boxcars with railroad section hands from Mexico in the early twentieth century.

Prominent in the repertoire of most Mexican-American storytellers I know is the legend of la Llorona, the weeping woman of Mexico. La Llorona, the story says, had a child she did not want. As for why she didn't want the child, the story varies, as is the way with folktales; some say the child's father was not the woman's husband. So she threw the child into the river.

In the next scene of the tale la Llorona arrived at the gates of heaven and was turned away by her saint, who told her she could not enter until she found her baby. So she returned to earth to search, and she has wandered the banks of the river ever since, seeking her baby and crying. "La Llorona" means "the Weeping One."

The wonderful part of this story is the way it has been localized, or changed to fit new places of residence. Today la Llorona wanders not only the watercourses of Mexico but also those of the United States—the Canadian, the Arkansas, the Cottonwood, the Platte. "My uncle was the good one for telling about the Llorona," said a woman in Emporia, Kansas. "We were such scaredy-cats anyway, we used to actually hear her cry."

The localization stretches the limits of credulity, even for a folktale. If la Llorona threw her baby into the river in Mexico, and now she is searching the Cottonwood or the Arkansas for it, then does she think that it floated upstream from the Gulf of Mexico? That sort of critical logic isn't important. Regardless of gravity, the logic of society said that la Llorona should be present in the new home in the United States.

Folktales, in addition to being entertainment, have purposes. They help people pass on their values to the next generation. The values conveyed through the legend of la

Llorona are simple and basic—that motherhood is sacred and that wrong will not go unpunished.

Folktales also may have more immediate uses, such as making children behave. La Llorona is present in all vicinities, and she is looking for a child; if she can't find her own, she will take another and try to sneak into heaven with it. Parents therefore advise their children not to roam far from home at night. Mothers especially call their children close when crossing a bridge, for surely la Llorona will be hiding underneath. "Te llevará la Llorona," they say—"La Llorona is going to get you"—and they don't have to worry about their children walking too close to the edge and falling in.—*TI*

3. *Corps of Engineers Legends*

THERE was a time when the Great Plains comprised a rural culture with rural institutions like country schools and rural folklore like folk singing. Today the plains have largely a town culture. It's hard to find an authentic folk singer, and other types of classic folklore, such as ethnic folktales, also are scarce, except among recent immigrants.

This doesn't mean that folklore on the plains has gone the way of courting by buggy or Saturday-night shopping in town. For instance, folktales still thrive on the plains, mostly in the form of what folklorists classify as "legends." A legend is a story that is told for truth but on close examination proves to have an element of the fantastic in it. The story passes for true narrative under circumstances that create a suspension of disbelief. The gathering of darkness around a lonely campfire might accomplish this. Or the consumption of alcohol.

One relatively new presence on the plains that has created a fine body of legends is the reservoir, stories about which I like to call "Corps of Engineers legends" because the construction activities of that agency made them possible. I first remember hearing a Corps of Engineers legend from a fishing buddy of mine named Bill Rein when we were both preteenagers. We were catching catfish at the tunnel outlet of the Kanopolis Dam near Ellsworth, Kansas, when Bill told me about a little boy who had been fishing at the site on an earlier date. This fellow was catching all sorts of fish when no one else was catching anything, and so someone finally asked him what he was using for bait. "Snapping worms," was his reply. An examination of the bait showed that the snapping worms were baby rattlesnakes, and of course the boy died horribly.

Snakes and horrible death were likewise central to another Corps of Engineers legend, the story of the unfortunate water skier. This person skied about the reservoir until he (or more commonly, she) tired and then dropped off into a secluded cove. There she was engulfed by cottonmouth water moccasins so numerous and angry that the people in the boat could not even recover the body. This story I've heard told about various reservoirs in the plains states. What's more, on a trip to West Virginia I heard it again. The teller there added a new wrinkle. The water skier was not immediately dispatched by the snakes. Instead she reached a hand toward someone in the boat, saying, "Be careful, I'm stuck in some barbed wire or something here, and it's sticking me."

My own favorite Corps of Engineers legend, probably because I am a catfisherman myself, usually begins with the proposition that there is something wrong with the dam, and the corps sends some divers down to check it out. The divers come back to the surface panic-stricken, saying that they are never going down there again. There are monster catfish down there, they say, so big they could easily eat a man. These monster catfish are so common in reservoirs of the central plains that I'm surprised the Kansas Fish and Game Commission hasn't yet identified them.

I wonder what you would use for bait to catch one of these behemoths. Snapping worms, perhaps?—*TI*

4. *Teenage Legends*

I HAVE HEARD Corps of Engineers legends told by plains
dwellers of all ages. Some kinds of legends, though, are peculiar to teenagers. Teenagers are great tellers of legends,
many of them concerning disgusting creatures that roam
the countryside looking for romantic youth in parked cars.
These creatures are bent on doing in one or both of the
would-be lovers. Folklorist Jan Brunvand has collected
these legends all over the United States.

I think the teenagers of the Great Plains have developed some legends indigenous to the region. My personal
favorite is the Hamburger Man of Hutchinson, Kansas.
Hutchinson folk say that the Hamburger Man was dis-
figured by some sort of accident that made his face look
like hamburger. The accident might have been a fire, a war
wound, or most fitting of all for Hutchinson, home of the
world's largest grain elevator, a grain-elevator explosion.

The Hamburger Man lives in a shack in the sandhills or
in a shack down by the state reformatory, either site being
pretty sinister. At night this miserable fellow roams the
sandhills in the Hutchinson vicinity, especially a site known
as Hamburger Hill. Sometimes he ranges as far away as
Nickerson.

What the Hamburger Man does to teenagers found
parked in the country is too horrible to relate. In his spare
time he also steals children and mutilates livestock. Sometimes he carries an ax with which to dispatch his victims.
Other times he has a hook in place of his right hand. Either way, this local character has a remarkable similarity to
other legendary figures found across the United States.

A favorite parking spot for teenagers in Topeka, Kansas, is the vicinity of Rochester Cemetery. The cemetery is
the haunt of a frightening spirit known as the Albino Lady.
During her earthly life the Albino Lady suffered cruel per-
secution for her physical oddity. Spiritually, she remains
pretty odd. Not only is she an albino, but she also dresses

entirely in white and, to top it all, carries a white poodle dog in her arms. Teenagers like to go to the cemetery to look for her. Younger children are afraid of her because she is said to steal children from schoolyards should they stay too late in the evening.

This business of stealing children makes the Albino Lady akin to the Mexican legendary figure, la Llorona. On the other hand, the Albino Lady also reminds me of a spooky feminine figure that my wife, Charlotte, has told me inhabits the cemeteries of West Germany. She is the Alt Weissen, which means "old Mrs. White," and she also likes to chase children. Her other talents include changing herself into butter or a cat.

I don't mean here to neglect the Caney River (Kansas) Wildman, the Ponca City (Oklahoma) Deer Woman, or the McLaughlin (South Dakota) Bigfoot, but the Hamburger Man and the Albino Lady are wonderful examples of teenage legends. How many such legendary creatures do we have on the Great Plains? And if they are this grisly in Hutchinson and Topeka, then what must they be in Amarillo or North Platte?—*TI*

5. *Legends of the Lone Highway*

DOWN a west Texas highway speeds a beer truck bound for its next delivery. The dozing driver starts awake to a fearful sight—a giant armadillo looming out of the mesquite and lumbering onto the asphalt. The angry creature bowls over the truck, leaves it disabled in the ditch, and disappears again into the mesquite.

This story of the giant armadillo, related to me by folks in Wichita Falls, is not folklore. It is rather a figment of an advertising campaign by a beer company (which frequently also promotes armadillo races).

The beer promoters are clever to root their advertisements in the legendary tradition of hazardous highway travel. Americans, particularly plains folk, are immensely mobile, and their propensity for travel has generated countless legends similar to the concocted one of the giant armadillo.

The antecedents of these stories reach at least as far back historically as the overland migration by way of the Oregon and California trails. Travelers up the Platte River road who became discouraged or spooked commonly returned east with the explanation that they had "seen the elephant."

Moreover, contemporary legends of the lone highway are not confined to the plains. Teenagers (by age or by temperament) across the country tell the story of the vanishing hitchhiker—a pretty girl who is picked up by a male driver but who disappears before reaching her announced destination; the driver subsequently learns that the girl had been killed in an accident years earlier. Or they tell the one of the runaway grandmother—a deceased family member whose body, carried in the luggage rack of a station wagon, is lost when the car is stolen.

Strange fare, these highway legends, but before dismissing them as teenagers' foolishness, consider that hundreds of southern Kansans have turned out over the years to search for the State Lake Snake. The State Lake Snake is a blacksnake about the size of a telephone pole. During the spring of the year he may be observed stretched across Highway 54, west of the town of Kingman, sunning himself.

One fellow says the State Lake Snake knocked him off his horse. Another says that he emptied his rifle into the creature's head, whereupon it wrapped its coils around its head and squeezed the bullets out.

The State Lake Snake may meet his match if he slithers a little farther south to the vicinity of Anthony, Kansas. Have you ever noticed dead animals along the road that almost look as though they have been skinned? Chances are they were victims of the Badger. The Badger prowls southern Kansas in search of animal prey, particularly dogs. When he catches them, he reaches inside them and turns them inside out. Jeff Masner, of Anthony, says, "When you see a dog's skin turned inside out, that's the Badger."

I think these highway legends are favorites because, like the armadillo story, they take things that drivers commonly encounter—snakes sunning themselves or road-killed animals—and turn them into something exciting. Highway traveling can be boring, after all, and a good scare relieves the tedium.

One scare that drivers hope to avoid is being stranded on the road at night. So don't drive up the ridge out of Sleepy Hollow, near Arkansas City, Kansas, at midnight. If you do, your engine will die. Should you disregard my warning, though, and it happens to you as I have said, then don't get out to hike, don't try to call the auto club—just stay in the car, set the brake, lock the doors, and wait for daylight. If you get out of the car, then I'm not responsible for what may happen.—*TI*

6. *Flathead Stories*

I've always admired the work and style of John Lomax, the west Texas farm boy who became America's foremost collector of ballads and folk songs. Late in his life Lomax recorded for the Library of Congress the story of how he discovered in Fort Worth the classic cowboy song "Old Chisholm Trail." He began, innocently, "One night I found myself in the back room of the White Elephant Saloon." In the spirit of John Lomax, then, here is how I discovered the best string of catfish stories I ever heard.

One night I happened to find myself in Carl's Bar, just a block off Main Street in Hutchinson, Kansas. A one-armed fat man at the bar was running out of money. Primed with free beers and gullible questions, he began pouring forth legends. Most of his fish stories I had heard before, but never told with such style and dispatch.

The subject of most of the stories was flathead catfish,

and the scene Kanopolis Reservoir, although, of course, it could just as well have been any of the multipurpose reservoirs of the plains. Those big flatheads, the one-armed man explained, grow to well over one hundred pounds and get so lazy that "they just lay there by the dam." He then recounted, as I have earlier, the story of the terrified skin divers who encountered those catfish.

And how about that water skier who disappeared? The one who fell from his skis and they never found the body. "But I know what happened to him," the old guy said. A flathead got him, pulled him right under.

"This friend" of his—it's always "this friend" who has such adventures—used to hand-fish or noodle flatheads in rivers. (Do I really need to finish this story? Don't you know how it's going to end?) The fellow reached under a log, felt this big flathead, and stuck his hand in its mouth. His arm went in all the way up to his shoulder, and when he tried to pull it out, the flathead chomped down. The hand fisherman fought loose, but the skin was torn from his whole arm.

The proper way to catch flatheads, as "this other friend" did up in Kanopolis, was with a trotline of steel cable fixed with hooks "about so big"—and here the one-armed guy laid his artificial forearm on the bar to show the steel hook with which it was fitted. Fingering the hook with his good hand, he told me how those big flatheads would straighten out the fishhooks "like that."

That hook business was the capper. I suppose if there were such a thing as a tale-telling contest, the rules would outlaw such props as this fellow's hook, but for freestyle spellbinding from a barstool, I never saw the like.

Neither had Jeff Masner, who came in and sat down just as the hook tale got under way. Jeff was the fellow who first told me about the notorious Anthony Badger that catches dogs and turns them inside out. Jeff soon adroitly turned the talk toward dogfights and "this friend" of the one-armed man who had a vicious Airedale that had whipped twelve straight pit bulldogs.

I suspected that this was a ploy on Jeff's part, a suspicion confirmed when he next introduced the subject of badgers. The one-armed man suddenly appeared more animated than ever. Badgers are misunderstood, he explained. People think that they fight with their claws, but they fight only with their teeth. Their claws are just for digging.

"Those badgers are pretty mean, aren't they?" Jeff inquired.

"Oh yeah—you know, they'll turn a dog inside out."—*TI*

7. *Cow Tipping and Snipe Hunting*

NOT too long ago one of my colleagues here at Emporia State University, knowing of my interest in folklore, handed me a newspaper clipping, a review of Lisa Birnbaum's latest book—a guide to colleges and universities. Birnbaum had received a decent amount of fame (and some nice royalties as well) from her earlier publication, *The Preppy Handbook.*

What had caught my colleague's eye was a reference in the review to cow tipping, a traditional folk prank, according to Birnbaum, at many nonurban universities. What is cow tipping? A lot like snipe hunting.

This is how it works: Some ornery upperclassmen grab a naïve freshman late at night and take him out into the middle of a pasture. There they force him to sneak up on a herd of standing, sleeping cows and give one a sharp push in the flank, thus causing her to fall over with a thud. Then they run like blazes because the cow gets to her feet very angry, looking for someone to chase.

I thought at first, not having had the opportunity to see the book itself, that the episode in the review might be a put-on. My colleague, however, said that he had seen Birnbaum on a late-night talk show, where guest and host appeared to take the matter quite seriously (or at least as seriously as such matters tend to be taken on late-night talk shows).

Now I don't want to sound like sour grapes just becaue my own university didn't make Birnbaum's book, but I have

some doubts about the validity of the research. It's hard
for me to have total confidence in a book that states un-
critically that students tiptoe around in cow pastures in the
middle of the night looking for a cow to shove over. I will
give the author credit for not being suckered into trying to
tip a cow herself, but I can't believe that she didn't ask someone—the Ag dean, a farmer, even some student union
cowboy—whether or not cows sleep standing up.

As I said earlier, this whole affair sounds a lot like snipe
hunting, that venerable rite of passage in which the inno-
cent are quite literally left holding the bag in the middle of
a dark night, waiting for their erstwhile hunting companions to drive the snipe to them. The tricksters, in the meantime, have already gone back to town, leaving the unfortunate dupes to walk in alone.

Snipe hunters, at least, eventually come to the conclusion that they have been had, something that doesn't seem
to have occurred to Birnbaum. She would have been well
advised to have done a little reading—say, Vance Ran-
dolph's classic on Ozark folklore, *We Always Lie to Strangers*.

In the plains region, it seems to me, we don't lie to
strangers so much as we let them lie to themselves. We let
people convince themselves that something is true—like
the west Texas courthouse whittlers who sit around talking,
just loudly enough to be overheard by an obnoxious greenhorn, about how Old Fred is paying $25 a head to have
Circle Bar cattle hunted up out of the brush and delivered
at the stockyards.

A couple of weeks later the greenhorn—scratched,
bruised, and broke—gets accused of rustling when Old
Fred sees some of his Circle Bars penned up as he drives
into town. Another greenhorn bites the dust.—*JH*

8.   *The Truth About Snipe Hunting*

I WISH my partner would stop talking about snipe hunting
as merely a hoax played upon the gullible. It happens that

I grew up in the vicinity of the Cheyenne Bottoms, one of those Great Plains marshes that serve as linchpins in the central waterfowl flyway. There is indeed a shorebird called the Wilson's, or common, snipe (some oldtimers call it the jacksnipe). It's a small, fast-flying, long-billed bird that makes a funny noise when it flies and would look a lot like a woodcock to you folks from forested country.

Snipe are migratory gamebirds, and as a boy I used to hunt them in marshy pastures. Their erratic flight makes the shooting tough, but it's easier to hit the most elusive snipe on the wing than it is to convince someone who has been an unwitting participant in a nighttime snipe-hunting expedition that I am serious when I talk about bagging one.

Indeed, here is a case where farce has displaced fact in folk life. I therefore have given up trying to legitimatize the idea of snipe hunting. Instead I have made the proposition a subject of study for some of my summer folklore classes.

Here is a question that I pose to students of folklore: What does a snipe look like? Perpetrators of snipe-hunting hoaxes have to make their stories believable, and their victims surely demand to know what sort of bird it is that they are pursuing. In response to this question David Woelk, a scholar from Hutchinson, Kansas, has made a notable discovery: the snipe adapts to its environment. In eastern Kansas, he has found, the snipe of legend, a long-billed, long-necked bird, roosts on the branches of trees. To catch one, you have to climb a tree and tap on a basket with a stick, which attracts the critter into the basket. That makes sense in forested country, I guess.

On the plains of Western Kansas, however, the snipe is a long-legged bird that runs down the rows of corn and milo at night. You have to hold your bag close to the ground and make a clicking sound with your mouth to get him to hop into the bag. Physically, the description of this bird sounds to me a lot like that of a ringneck pheasant.

Now comes another student of mine who was a participant in a snipe hunt in southern Idaho. She says the long-legged bird described to her dwelt out among the sagebrush, ran fast, and, upon later reflection, sounds for all the world like a roadrunner.

What all this means, I think, is that, even in respect to the most ludicrous human endeavors, we are creatures of place. Even the things that we conjure in our imaginations are products of our immediate surroundings. That's what makes people on the plains Plains Folk.—*TI*

9. *Water Witching*

ANY serious student of folklore soon discovers that science and folkways coexist only uneasily—that where science can advance with certainty, technology and the folk traditions tied to it must follow. What about areas where science cannot speak with positive assurance? This is the sort of foggy domain where folk belief reigns.

Water witching is an example. Since at least the early 1500s, when Martin Luther condemned it as a violation of the First Commandment, water witching has continued to command the confidence of many people. This practice is truly traditional. Water witches learn their craft by observing and imitating others; then they pass it along to another generation.

Such was the case with Ola Pracht, a water witch with whom I visited ("witching," incidentally, is the customary word for the practice in America, more common than either "dowsing" or "divining"). Ola and her husband, Fred, live in the Cottonwood valley near Cedar Point, Kansas. Ola first witched water about twenty years ago after watching a well driller, Ernest Lespagnard, witch a location on her place.

I recognized the name, "Lespagnard," as French, which got me a little excited. I knew that water witching was and is a strong belief in France, where there are professional societies devoted to its perpetuation and improvement. I also knew that substantial numbers of French immigrants had settled along the upper Cottonwood. Sure enough, Fred and Ola recalled that another fellow of French descent, Ernest Lalouette, also witched.

The common tool of the water witch is a wishbone-shaped green stick gripped in an uncomfortable, palms-up fashion. Peach is the generally preferred stock, but willow also is good. I watched Ola witch with elm, peach orchards having become scarce. She even uses a pair of pliers in a pinch.

They all nose-dive for her to indicate the location of water. How does it work? Like most other water witches, Ola cannot explain it exactly. Fred says, "She has a lot of electricity in her body."

That the Continental custom of water witching traveled to America with European immigrants is obvious. Its practice here was subject to the limitations and opportunities of the environment. In many parts of the plains, for instance, water witching was a useless craft. Where I grew up, in the Arkansas valley of Barton County, Kansas, you could drive a point anywhere and draw water, water witch or no water witch.

Elsewhere it was just as certain that there was no hope of hitting water-bearing sands, and in still other places the water-bearing stratum was defined and known to all—making water witching superfluous in either case.

In such a locality as the one where the Prachts live, an area of limestone hills, water-well drilling is a hit-or-miss affair. Geologists can cite the chances of hitting good water in a particular vicinity, but they cannot drive a stake in the ground, say, "Drill here," and guarantee a good well. The willingness of water witches to do just that is their great allure.

Surely in the expanse of the North American plains, with all the various cultural groups settled upon them, and all the different geological conditions characterizing their localities, water witching must flourish with countless variations and idiosyncrasies. But that's what makes it folklore—there isn't a "right" way of doing it.—*TI*

10. *Rain Follows the Plow*

MYTHS, most modern Americans would say, were the pagan beliefs of ancient peoples. They don't exist in our enlightened nation.

Wrong. A myth is just a belief, true or false, general enough and powerful enough to excite emotions and motivate action. We have plenty of them, and some of the notable ones are concerned with the Great Plains.

To begin with, Thomas Jefferson and his contemporaries included our region in the mythical land they referred to as the Great Interior Valley. Jefferson, believing that agriculture was the only truly virtuous occupation, intended that the United States should forever remain a nation of farmers. That was why he bought the Louisiana Territory from France. The Great Interior Valley, he believed, was so vast and so productive that America need never close up its people in factories.

The trouble with this idea was that it ran into another developing belief—the myth of the Great American Desert. Originating with the reports of such explorers as Meriwether Lewis, Zebulon Pike, and Stephen Long, and feeding upon eastern Americans' distaste for open country, the myth of the desert was imprinted in the minds and the geography texts of a generation of Americans. The plains, they said, were unfit for cultivation and suitable only as a refuge for wandering Indians.

So long as there was agricultural land available in the Mississippi valley or on the Pacific slope, the Great American Desert might bake in peace. By the 1870s, though, homesteaders were testing it and railroads dissecting it. It was time for a new myth, one that would reinstate the Great Plains in the Great Interior Valley.

Four words summed it up: "Rain Follows the Plow." Simple optimism was the origin of the new myth. After but brief experience, settlers were wont to say, "The country is getting more seasonable." Blatant propagandists, such as railroad land agents, confirmed that the very act of breaking the sod was wreaking a meteorological revolution by releasing humidity into the air. It was unthinkable that divine omnipotence should have created a useless land and not given man the instrument with which to transform it. "The plow will go forward," pronounced Charles Dana Wilber of Nebraska. "God speed the plow."

The promoters got help from Ferdinand V. Hayden of the U.S. Geological Survey, who surveyed the western territories during the 1870s. Always one to see the good in the bleakest landscape, he won the title of the "businessman's geologist."

Scientific underpinning came from a University of Nebraska professor named Samuel Aughey. He said that the turning of sod and the growth of crops increased the evaporative surface, resulting in more humidity and more rain. The plains, he predicted, were soon to become as lush and tropical as they had been in the prehistoric past. This sort of geological analysis put Aughey, a biologist, on shaky ground, but promoters nevertheless quoted him continually.

Plains dwellers who lived through the drought of the late 1880s and the early 1890s mocked the myth that "Rain Follows the Plow." The myth ought to be dead, but I find that it is just latent, waiting to spring back to life. With groups of students, and in casual conversation, I have experimented by poker-facedly presenting the idea that since farmers have filled the plains the climate is much less desertlike than it was. Heads nod; plenty of people are still willing to believe.—*TI*

11.   *Tree Claims*

"RAIN FOLLOWS THE PLOW"—that notable American myth—had a companion belief not so easily summarized in a catchy phrase. This was the idea that the presence of trees would make a place more rainy. Here was a myth powerful

enough that it found expression in an act of Congress and
left an imprint on the plains that persists to the present day.

The belief that trees increased precipitation evolved in
a manner similar to the idea that rain follows the plow. Scientific theory, selfish promotion, and popular hopes spun
a web of presumption, the threads of which generally ran
in one of two directions. One was that trees stopped the
wind and thereby prevented moisture evaporated out of
the soil from blowing away. The foliage diverted the water
vapor upward. It soon accumulated and fell back to earth
as rain.

The other line of thought involved electricity. Rain
clouds, it was said, were full of positive charges. Trees were
fine conductors of electricity and offered a great surface
upward toward the clouds. The trees, then, would act as
magnets and pull rain clouds toward them.

This was not just the idle talk of crackpots. Joseph
Wilson, commissioner of the U.S. General Land Office, believed it. The Smithsonian Institution and the U.S. Geological Survey supported it. Dakota Territory and the state
of Nebraska both passed laws giving tax breaks to tree
planters, and the new state of South Dakota even granted
free land to those who would grow trees upon it.

It was not a surprise, then, when Congress in 1873 enacted the Timber Culture Act. This curious statute provided that a settler might receive patent to 160 acres from
the public domain if he planted 40 acres in trees and nurtured them for ten years. Senator Phineas Hitchcock of
Nebraska made it clear that Congress passed the act "not
merely for the value of the timber itself, but for its influence upon the climate."

The Timber Culture Act, most agree, was a failure.
Settlers found it difficult to keep trees alive on the plains,
and so in 1878 Congress reduced the requirements under
the act to ten acres of plantings containing "675 living
thrifty trees" (whatever a "thrifty" tree is) at the time of patent. Worse, the act seemed to promote fraud. Countless
speculators took claims, did not even pretend to fulfill the
act's requirements, and nevertheless received their patents.

In 1883 the prestigious *Nation* magazine announced that the Timber Culture Act "has failed deplorably . . . to accomplish what was honestly expected of it." Congress waited until 1891, after drought had enveloped the plains and its infant groves, to repeal the act.

Even if the act failed to deliver what was expected of it, people on the plains still cannot view it as a silly anachronism. Many of our ancestors, by honest means or otherwise, used it to acquire a quarter section. Some of them even managed to grow trees on the land, although they had trouble getting government officials to recognize the species they planted—such as Osage orange, hackberry, or cottonwood—as genuine "timber" trees.

What has become of the groves established under the Timber Culture Act? Where do they survive, and what sort of shape are they in? I suspect that many have been important not only as shelterbelts and wildlife covers but also as social centers for picnics and other gatherings. Consider your own locality, if you live on the plains; isn't there a grove of trees that serves as the site for community events?—*TI*

12.   *Red River Valley*

A CHANCE MEETING with Mrs. Marion Kestl, of Salina, Kansas, started me in pursuit of the origins of a classic folk song of the Great Plains, "Red River Valley." Mrs. Kestl showed me a manuscript ballad book that her mother, Libbie Reed, had compiled in 1896, when she was living in Hay Springs, Nebraska. Various details of the style in which the songs are inscribed show that they were written down from memory, not copied from published works. The repertoire that Libbie Reed recorded in 1896 contains an interesting mix of parlor songs and folk songs.

Among them is "The Loup River Valley," a Nebraska sandhills variant of "Red River Valley." With apologies to readers in Texas, I'd like to show where "The Loup River Valley" fits into the history of folk song on the plains.

Most residents of the southern plains assume that the Red River valley to which the folksong refers is the valley of the stream that forms the boundary between Texas and Oklahoma. So also assumed such great folklorists as Carl Sandburg and John Lomax, who traced the origins of what they knew as a cowboy song to a parlor song published in New York and called "The Bright Mohawk Valley." The New York song, however, appears to have been only another local variant of an earlier song, a "Red River Valley" spawned upon the Red River of the North, which forms the boundary between North Dakota and Minnesota and then flows on north into Canada and Lake Winnipeg.

In 1869 the residents of the lower reaches of the valley of the Red River of the North revolted against the imposition upon them of the authority of the central Canadian government. The occupants of the valley were métis, the offspring of French traders and native Indians. They were accustomed to the jurisdiction of the commercial Hudson's Bay Company and feared the government of Canada, a creation of the British crown.

From British soldiers who suppressed the Red River Rebellion came the song "Red River Valley," about a métis girl mourning the departure of a British soldier with whom she had fallen in love. This song, well known in Canada, percolated into the United States, where people unfamiliar with its history changed its plot. In the "Red River Valley" sung on the southern plains, the protagonist is a cowboy trying to persuade his sweetheart not to leave the territory. The roles of male and female have been reversed from those in the Canadian folk song.

To get back to Libbie Reed's Loup valley version—it also has the genders reversed from the Canadian situation, but the male figure in the song is not a cowboy, just a local boy. It concludes with his plea that, if his darling will not have him, she at least might stay in the valley and find a husband among the many bachelors there, "young men and widowers, too," one of whom must be "good enough for you."

So "Loup River Valley" stands as partial proof that "Red River Valley" is much more than a folk song of Texas cowboys and that, in fact, the Texas cowboy version is only a branch of a tree rooted in Canada and stretching the length of the plains.—*TI*

13. *Home on the Range*

J IM and I once made a presentation of Great Plains folk-songs to a banquet group in Scott City, Kansas. At the conclusion a peculiar thing happened. We began our usual closing number, "Home on the Range," and as if it were the national anthem, everyone in the audience stood up to join in the singing.

"Home on the Range" is, of course, the state song of Kansas, so designated by the legislature in 1947. It may offend some Texans to point out that the song originated in northern Kansas. It does offend me to hear this fine old folk song so often made fun of as corny. That's why I was so impressed with the folks in Scott City. They are patriots.

"Home on the Range" is a song of the plains, not of a particular state. It is a genuine folk song, not the slick ditty of a Tin Pan Alley composer, not the shallow fluff of a self-serving booster. The text originated with an obscure folk poet—Dr. Brewster Higley, a country doctor on the farmers' frontier of Smith County, Kansas. Higley had been widowed three times, had been divorced once, and evidently made frequent resort to alcohol. His appreciation of the Great Plains landscape was nevertheless profound, and in 1872 he expressed it in his poem, known early as "Western Home."

Higley's poem, set to music by a local musician, Dan Kelley, became a favorite of string bands at get-togethers in the Solomon Valley. Residents there liked its references to the Solomon River and to Beaver Creek. They passed the song along to trail-riding cowboys, who carried it back home with them to Texas. The cowboys substituted Texas for Kansas as the setting for the song and incorporated in it their own beloved Red River. John Lomax, the folklorist from the University of Texas, eventually rediscovered the song we know as "Home on the Range" from the oral tradition. He learned it from a black saloonkeeper in San Antonio and printed it in his book *Cowboy Songs and Other Frontier Ballads,* published in 1910. Recorded renditions of the song that became enormously popular during the 1930s (Franklin Roosevelt said it was his favorite song) were based on the Lomax text.

Kansas partisanship aside, the truth is that Higley's poem, with its mention of poisonous herbage growing and life streams buoyantly flowing, was pretentious and awkward. Oral circulation in the cowboy tradition improved it, stripping away the fluff but retaining the best of its sentiments and imagery. It is the imagery—picture a lone figure under the glittering stars, antelope flocks among white rocks and green hillsides, swans on a sandy river—that leads me to pronounce "Home on the Range" the finest piece of lyric folk poetry ever to grace the culture of the North American plains.

There are other reasons for respecting this folk song. Its melody is fitting, cast in simple ¾ time, the signature that comes naturally to folk singers in evocation of the Great Plains landscape. And as both a historian and an outdoorsman, I appreciate the song as a document of environmental history. Higley stood on the cutting edge of the farmers' frontier, looked upon the open range, and recorded what forms of life pioneers in the region considered notable—the whitetail deer, the pronghorn antelope, the buffalo, the long-billed curlew (a long-legged, hook-billed migratory bird, now rare), the trumpeter swan, and the many wildflowers.

The very frontier of settlement of which Higley was representative was to displace most of these creatures from common range on the plains. Higley's recording of their presence was evidence that even in his times, when pioneers struggled so hard against what seemed a hostile environment, at least some of them still had a sort of reverence for the environs through which they were passing.

So more power to you Scott Cityans, and to all you other plains people who aren't afraid to show respect for a true anthem of the plains.—*TI*

Part Two

FELLOW CREATURES OF
THE PLAINS

14. *Hopperdozers*

GRASSHOPPER infestations have been chronic and severe on the Great Plains, mainly for environmental reasons. Grasshoppers thrive where there is undisturbed grassland for nesting in conjunction with productive cropland for feeding. The plains, with a mixed economy of crops and stock raising, are grasshopper heaven, especially during dry years that give the little hoppers a chance to hatch out.

Farmers, desperate in the face of the infestations of the 1870s, 1890s, and 1930s, tried fires, nets, ditches, and all manner of strange inventions to combat the grasshoppers. Of these inventions the only one to enjoy a broad measure of usage, if not success, was the hopperdozer.

According to the research of R. Douglas Hurt, currently assistant director of the Missouri Historical Society but a native of Kansas, numerous farmer-inventors of the plains filed patents for grasshopper harvesters during the 1870s. Some crushed the insects between rollers, others mashed them between revolving knives, and one used near Abilene, Kansas, sucked them up like a vacuum cleaner.

About the same time various folk inventors independently developed what came to be known as the hopperdozer. A man named Lorenzo B. Canfield, of Syracuse, Nebraska, patented one, but he could not defend the patent, because others already had built basically the same device. The courts were right in that decision; I have read enough newspaper accounts from scattered localities to show that hopperdozers of folk origin were in use all over the plains.

The hopperdozer was a sort of sledge pulled or pushed by a team. The base of it was a pan or reservoir filled with coal oil. Sometimes the reservoir had dividers in it to make separate pans and keep the oil from all running to one end on sloping ground. Rising vertically from the back of the pan was a barrier of screen, cloth, or tarpaper.

The idea of the contraption was that the grasshoppers would jump up in front of it, hit the barrier, and die when they fell into the coal-oil reservoir. Once in a while the operator had to stop to clean out the grasshoppers and add more coal oil. Some operators then burned the resulting piles of hoppers.

The hopperdozer was best used in fields of alfalfa or young wheat. Obviously, dragging it through a field of mature wheat or growing corn destroyed the crop just as effectively as would the grasshoppers. There is no doubt that hopperdozers killed grasshoppers, but the insects usually moved in again quickly from neighboring acreage.

Still, during the 1930s hopperdozers again came into fairly common use. County agent reports show that in 1936 W. T. Ball built and used a mule-powered hopperdozer on his farm north of Emporia, Kansas. It had a corrugated tin barrier, but in every other way it was like those used in the 1870s.

In 1937 A. J. McCabe, from near Cottonwood Falls, Kansas, brought the hopperdozer into the automotive age. He fastened the pan and tarpaper barrier onto the front bumper of his Model A and drove it through his alfalfa fields. Measuring with a bucket, McCabe found that in an hour's work he killed two bushels of grasshoppers.

By this time, though, the use of arsenic bran against grasshoppers was foreshadowing the day of the use of chemical pesticides instead of mechanical devices to combat insects. In fact, back home on the farm we still have an arsenic-bran spreader used by my Granduncle Alvin at about this time. That's another story.—*TI*

15. *More Hopperdozers*

IN MAY, of 1985, I displayed some historical photographs at the Kansas Folklife Festival. The photographs that got the most attention were three from the 1930s: Dick Truitt bulldogging a full-grown bison, Mattie Downs (eight and one-half months pregnant) riding a bronc, and a hopperdozer. Not many people (in fact, nobody) could tell me any stories about bison dogging or pregnant lady bronc riders, but I did pick up quite a few accounts of hopperdozers.

Herbert Funk, of Marion, Kansas, built an interesting hopperdozer in the later 1930s. He took an old Studebaker pickup, shortened the wheel base by about a foot and a half, and reversed the differential so it would run backwards. Then he mounted a buck rake on it with a tin backdrop (about five feet high), placed two pans in the bottom of the backdrop (each pan about two feet wide, four inches deep, and six feet long, to fit the twelve-foot buck rake), and filled them with a mixture of water and used crankcase oil. He would drive through his fifteen-acre alfalfa field, usually in July and August when the insects were mature, getting three or four bushels of hoppers each time. Funk also used his motor-driven buck rake to carry loose hay to the overshot stacker during hay season, only he told me that they called it a go-devil when they were haying. (At home we always called ours, which my grandfather drove with a team of mules, a go-devil, although "buck rake" is another common term for the same device.)

James Schroll, who lived at Syracuse, Kansas, in the 1930s, recalled that the hopperdozer his father built also was mounted on a buck rake and had the pans filled with an oil-water mixture, but it was pulled by a team of horses.

Like Schroll, Jack Barba lived on the High Plains as a boy, and he remembers that his father, Martin, built and used a hopperdozer near Brighton, Colorado, in the mid-1930s. Some twelve feet wide, five feet deep, and about five feet high, it was made of corrugated tin roofing mounted on four-by-four skids. As with the others, the pans were filled with water and crankcase oil (most of the ones Tom wrote about earlier used coal oil), and the contraption was pulled by two horses, one on each side, and each led by hand.

The Barbas had several small alfalfa fields watered by ditch irrigation. They would straddle the irrigation ditches with the hopperdozer in the early morning, then circle the edges of the fields, figuring that grasshoppers always started at the outside of a field and worked their way in. As the pans filled up, the Barbas would scoop the dead hoppers into gunny sacks and throw the gunny sacks into washes to help stop erosion.

That use strikes me as fitting, if ironic—making a destructive pest serve as an agent of conservation.—*JH*

16. *Lunching on Locusts*

AFTER I had written an essay about hopperdozers on the plains, Paul W. Riegert, of the University of Regina, Saskatchewan, wrote to report a peculiar entomological development in his province. It seems a local entrepreneur struck a deal with a firm in Japan to catch grasshoppers in Canada and ship them to the island nation, there to be deep-fried for human consumption. The fellow made a prototype hopper-catcher that didn't work, and the whole affair amounted to little, except that it reminded me that people had considered something similar a century earlier.

In 1875, just after the great grasshopper year of 1874, a correspondent of the *Prairie Farmer* proposed that residents of the region infested with the insects turn the plague to their own advantage by promoting use of the creatures as food. He pointed out that ancient sculptures depicted humans eating and selling locusts, that the Book of Leviticus referred to them as clean meat, and that Europeans in India ate the insects curried. The writer himself had experimented with grasshoppers boiled, baked, fried in lard, and cooked in their own juices (think about that, all you folks who have held a grasshopper and had him spit tobacco juice on you). The fellow dried the hoppers in cakes for use through the winter. Suggesting that some butter and a little mint seasoned them nicely, he reported the insects had a distinctive taste that could be cultivated. Grasshopper soup, he said, was similar to crawfish bisque.

If other people in the region ever ate grasshoppers, I am not aware of it. Poultry and hogs, though, loved them. During infestations of both the nineteenth and the twentieth centuries, farmers employed grasshopper catchers and then fed the catch to the animals. The U.S. Department of Agriculture in 1919 issued plans for a sledge trap similar to a hopperdozer, to be dragged by two horses. Instead of falling into coal oil, the hoppers that hit the thing rolled down a piece of tin into a trap. Experts advised that grasshoppers were high in protein and would improve the laying of hens; they might even be dried for a winter poultry ration.

More commonly, people just turned poultry loose to feast on the insects in the field. Turkeys were especially enthusiastic predators of grasshoppers. Some folks who didn't want their chickens to range freely after the insects nailed boards and wire together into a portable run that could be placed out where the hoppers were thick and periodically moved to new areas of infestation.

The indirect effects of grasshopper plagues on poultry were not always good, however. In a shed on the family farm we have an old arsenic-bran spreader that my Granduncle Alvin bought to kill hoppers during the 1930s. It is basically a tub mounted on a broadcaster. My cousin Bernice recalls riding in the back of a pickup while Alvin made the rounds of his alfalfa fields with this spreader hitched behind.

The effectiveness of arsenic bran against grasshoppers varied with a number of factors, including the temperature; sometimes it was so hot that grasshoppers were reluctant to sit on the scorching earth to eat the bran. One thing is sure, though: the stuff killed anything that did eat it. My father told me that Uncle Alvin's turkeys got into some poison left in the spreader, and it was deadly.—*TI*

17. *Hessian Flies*

ENTOMOLOGISTS say that the Hessian fly, perhaps the worst insect pest in the history of North American wheat farming, is rampant again. The story of how this insect came to our continent, became a menace, and then was brought under control is a good study in how scientists and citizens can cooperate against such a problem.

Popular belief about the origin of the fly—that it came to America in the pallets of German "Hessian" mercenaries during the American Revolution—is a delight to a folklorist like me. The basis for this assumption was that the fly first was noticed on Long Island during Revolutionary times after Hessian troops had encamped there. I think the true origin of this belief, though, was the natural inclination of most folks to assume that evils which appear at the same time must be related somehow, through the hand of God or politicians or some other inscrutable power.

The Hessian fly crossed the continent with the frontier of wheat culture, reaching the west coast by the 1880s. Its greatest destructiveness was in the wheat belt of the Great Plains. During the early twentieth century, scientists blamed the insect for an average annual loss of 10 percent of the wheat crop in the United States. Localities sometimes suffered total loss.

The first step in controlling the Hessian fly was to determine its life cycle. This was a preoccupation with agricultural scientists at the turn of the century—the understanding of the life histories of pests so as to know how to combat them. They learned that the Hessian fly had a basic annual cycle of two generations, with extra generations in between during favorable years. In winter-wheat country, one generation got started in fall-sown plants, overwintered in them as larvae, and emerged in the spring as insects resembling mosquitoes. They spawned the next generation of larvae, which made their homes in the wheat stalks, remaining in the stubble after harvest. Flies from these larvae deposited eggs on another crop in the fall. The difference in the cycle in spring-wheat country was that the insects had no fall-sown crop to harbor them and thus had to overwinter in stubble or in volunteer wheat.

Farmers observed the damage, if not the physiological development, of the flies. Young plants failed to develop proper stems, and mature plants lodged, thereby destroying the crop.

Knowing these things, scientists advised logical measures. Farmers, they said, should plow early and deep to turn under the larvae in the stubble, destroy volunteer wheat, and prepare a good seedbed. Most important, they should plant winter wheat late enough in the fall that the summer generation of flies would have emerged and died before wheat came up. Some authorities even advised wheat growers to sow a few decoy strips of wheat to attract flies early in the fall and then to turn them under before sowing their crop.

Cooperation of the entire community was necessary to make this scheme work. Extension officials and editors publicized the "fly-free" dates that applied to various localities—late October in northern Oklahoma, for instance, but October 1 in southern Nebraska. If everyone observed the fly-free date, the Hessian fly disappeared.

Entomologists now advise generally the same controls. The only difference today is that there are improved fly-resistant varieties of wheat.

As the Hessian fly resurges, we will see whether community cooperation again can be rallied to suppress it.—*TI*

18. *Chinch-Bug Barriers*

THE chinch bug is a hungry and persistent creature. He sleeps in the winter in clumps of grass, but spring finds him munching on small grain crops. Once these are gone, in June he crawls out of the stubble and into any green, growing feed he can find, soon toppling stalks of corn, milo, or, in days past, kaffir.

Before the advent of chemical pesticides (and these have by no means whipped the chinch bug), farmers and experimenters tried various means to stop the migration of chinch bugs and save feed crops. Winter burning of the insects' grassy havens might reduce the numbers, but suppose a farmer discovered an infestation in the summer?

An early response was the dust barrier. The farmer cut a lister furrow between the stubble where the bugs originated and the feed that they sought. Then he pulverized the dirt in the furrow by dragging a log up and down it. This was often a boy's job, and many an old-timer has told me his miserable memories of riding a horse up and down the furrow, dragging a log. In time farmers replaced the log with a little sledge that had two boards fitted in a V underneath to run along the furrow.

The chinch bugs hated to crawl into the dust, and so the barrier worked—until it rained. Then, unless the farmer quickly restored the dust barrier, the bugs crossed it. Crude oil poured along the line sometimes improved the effectiveness but was not foolproof.

So during the mid-1920s extension officials counseled farmers to construct barriers of creosote oil and calcium cyanide. The first step in this method was to plow a furrow between the stubble and the field, throwing the dirt away from the bug-infested stubble. Next the farmer punched a hole in the bottom of a bucket, which he filled with creosote. Up the furrow he walked, spewing a line of creosote on top of the dirt thrown out of the furrow. Along the creosote line the farmer dug postholes about a rod apart and about a foot deep. In each hole he placed a spoonful of cyanide.

To understand the effectiveness of this creosote-cyanide barrier, put yourself in the place of the chinch bug. He crawls out of the stubble and springs for some tasty corn or kaffir, scrambling through a furrow only to run up against a line of stinky creosote. He turns to the left or right and follows the line, looking for a place to cross. Suddenly he topples into a hole and dies of cyanide poisoning.

The barrier worked if the farmer cleaned out the dead bugs and put in new cyanide periodically, laid down wings of creosote to guide the bugs into the postholes, and renewed the creosote line daily. He didn't have to get out too early in the day, since the bugs didn't begin moving until midafternoon.

I suppose this was all right for protecting a few piddling acres of feed, but maintaining such a barrier around large fields would have been a hot and tedious job. The chinch-bug barrier belongs to the era of labor-intensive farming, when there were always some boys around the place that could be assigned such drudgery.

Still, there was no part of the operation that could not be mechanized and performed handily today. Creosote chinch-bug barriers worked. Why couldn't you mount a contraption on your pickup bumper to lay one down speedily?—*TI*

19. *Screwworms*

SCREWWORMS—maybe the word didn't strike terror in the hearts of Great Plains ranchers, but it certainly filled them with anxiety, dismay, and frustration. The screwworm season varied with warm weather—a long season for the southern plains, short for the north—but when it hit, it had definite consequences.

For one thing, all working of cattle was strictly limited to the colder, nonfly-infested months. Kansas calves, for instance, born in April stayed bulls until October. Yearling stockers bought in May kept their horns until fall. Another effect was that calves born in the summer months had to be carefully watched for screwworms in the navel. In fact, the entire herd had to be closely looked after, for a small wire cut, if infested, could result in a debilitated animal—or a dead one.

Screwworms were the larval stage of the screwworm fly. Besides doing serious damage, they were undoubtedly one of the most repulsive sights a stockman would ever encounter: a packed, squirming, stinking, whitish-colored mass.

Treatments varied. With our stock we used a commercial product, KRS. It must have had a creosote base; its strong penetrating odor could last for months if you spilled some on your boots. I haven't seen a can of KRS for years, but I can still smell it! Actually, I liked a faint odor of KRS, and still do, but most people hated it.

Other people used turpentine or kerosene instead of a commercial treatment. Some thought that each worm needed to be picked out, but my father thought that squirting them up good with KRS would do the job. Too much picking around and the wound would be irritated and thus encourage reinfestation.

Surely the most unusual folk method for getting rid of screwworms was practiced in parts of Texas earlier in the century. Some people there had the reputation of being able to "talk" screwworms out of an infected animal, even if the cow was miles away. Gabriel García Márquez, the renowned Latin American novelist, says that he saw a man in Colombia "say a prayer over a cow with worms in its ear, and the worms fell out." It sounds a little like witchcraft or voodoo, but probably it was just coincidence. Sometimes an animal would lose the worms as they matured and at the same time not have any new eggs deposited, thus making the "magic" appear to work.

Today screwworms are nearly forgotten in the central and northern plains, and they are not much of a problem in the Southwest, thanks to a government eradication program that began a couple of decades ago. Male screwworm flies were sterilized by radiation and then released to mate. The resulting sterile eggs have, over the years, reduced the screwworm to a minor annoyance.

Vigilance is still required, but the program is an outstanding success, saving the livestock industry millions of dollars each year. Farmers and ranchers often have bad things to say about government programs and policies, but in at least this one instance they were delighted with a little interference from Washington.—*JH*

20. *Rabbit Drives*

In the winter of 1981–82 citizens of Idaho sought to rid themselves of voracious white-tailed jackrabbits by staging rabbit drives in which they clubbed thousands of the creatures to death. The scenes in Idaho were reminiscent of many such events on the eastern side of the Rockies, on the Great Plains, where during drought years black-tailed jackrabbits can become a serious pest.

Jackrabbits tend to overmultiply during a series of dry years, presumably because of low mortality rates for baby bunnies during sunny weather. Some biologists refer to the jackrabbit as a sort of "animal weed" that flourishes when times are worst. I dimly recall witnessing a rather poorly organized rabbit drive when I was growing up during the filthy fifties, but from newspaper accounts I gather that the greatest rabbit drives of all must have been during the mid-1930s.

The basic idea of a rabbit drive was simple. Hundreds, even thousands, of participants surrounded the area to be driven, which ranged upward from two sections. Whooping and waving, carrying clubs, they moved toward the center of the drive area, pushing the frightened rabbits before them.

In the center of the drive was a pen, usually constructed of chicken wire. From an opening in the pen stretched out two lines of snowfence forming a V. The object was to drive the rabbits through the V and into the pen.

Then the shouting began and the hair flew, as the excited drivers swung broomsticks and baseball bats. When the slaughter was over, farmers usually hauled off the dead rabbits to feed hogs or chickens.

The most successful rabbit drive I know of took place near Dighton, Kansas, on Sunday afternoon, February 10, 1935. Drivers reportedly numbering 10,000 covered an area eight miles square—sixty-four sections—and killed some 35,000 jackrabbits.

These rabbit drives were great social events. Local chapters of the Farm Bureau, the American Legion, the Lions Club, and the Chamber of Commerce were common sponsoring organizations. Communities vied with one another to stage the biggest drives and to tell the tallest tales of them afterward.

In Idaho recently and on the plains decades ago, the rabbit drives drew plenty of criticism from humane-society types. But as a farmer from Kalvesta, Kansas, explained in 1935, "You wouldn't feel any pity for these rabbits if you had to make your living out of the ground."

It's hard to find too much fault with a method of pest control that kills the pests, harms no beneficial creatures, leaves no residual chemicals, and serves a social purpose.—*TI*

21. *Catching Live Jackrabbits*

JACKRABBIT populations tend to rise and fall across the plains, and as nearly as I can tell right now the count is fairly low. In the past few months I've had the chance to cover quite a bit of the Great Plains (traveling by car from here in Emporia, Kansas, to Bismarck, North Dakota, on one trip; to Canyon, Texas, on another), and I don't think I saw more than three or four jacks altogether.

In fact, the most jackrabbits I have seen recently were in Lane County, Kansas. We must have seen a dozen per mile for several miles as we drove through late one night about a year ago. I still see an occasional jack here in the Flint Hills, too, but they are not nearly as numerous as they were when I was younger.

I got to thinking about all this a couple of nights ago when I ran into an old friend with whom I had once participated in a very unusual jackrabbit hunt—catching them alive. The friend was Don Berger, and I had gone along with him and his father (Marlin), his brothers (Kenny and Bobby), and several others one night more than twenty years ago.

Marley Berger was a trader—he'd buy or sell anything that breathed and lots of things that didn't. Somehow or other he had found out that greyhound racers were paying good money (three dollars each) for live jackrabbits, and one thing he had plenty of on his farm near Halstead, Kansas, was jackrabbits.

Catching them was the tricky part. It was a nighttime operation that required a car, a hand-held spotlight, a .22 rifle, and a net. One person drove the car around a country road, out across a field of wheat stubble, or through a pasture. When a rabbit started up, then paused, Marley would drive as close to it as he dared while the spotlight holder kept the rabbit blinded. At this point the rifleman would fire a bullet just above the rabbit's head, temporarily deafening it (or so the theory went). The netter would then step off the running board of the pickup and, with both hands, slam the net over the temporarily dazed (or at least distracted) rabbit.

I know. I wouldn't have believed it either. But I saw it happen.

Some of the rabbits went to Abilene, Kansas (a major racing greyhound center and home of the Greyhound Hall of Fame), but most were sent east—to trainers in Tennessee, Kentucky, and Florida. Each rabbit was shipped individually in a small boxlike crate; two rabbits in the same container would fight and kill each other. Also, the box could not be too large or the rabbit would run against the sides and kill or injure itself. The only provision was half an apple, which provided all the food and moisture necessary for the trip.

Rabbits were usually shipped in lots of one hundred, and the buyers paid the freight, so each shipment brought in a tidy three hundred preinflation dollars, less expenses. With the usual bag for a night's hunt ranging from fifty to a hundred rabbits and expenses limited to a few gallons of twenty-seven-cent gasoline and some .22 shells, those were pretty good wages.

Good enough that Marley didn't have too much patience with any guest hunter who shot low. One dead rabbit and the rifle went back to someone with a better aim than I had.—*JH*

22. *Pest Contests*

THE story of jackrabbit drives on the plains illustrates to me that organized community efforts to combat animal pests inevitably take on a measure of epic absurdity. For instance, does anyone else besides me remember FFA pest contests?

Pest contests were sponsored in high schools by the Future Farmers of America. Each pest was assigned a point value—so many points for a sparrow (not many for just a sparrow), more for a starling, and an enormous number for a rat. Other pests carrying point values were pigeons, crows, mice, skunks, and coyotes. The FFA members divided into teams and chose captains, and the team accumulating the most points within a specified time won.

I wasn't yet in high school when this was going on (the 1950s and 1960s), but I was involved because my brothers were FFA members. The FFA boys soon figured out that the best way to rack up a lot of points was to hunt on cold winter nights. Then the starlings and sparrows would be roosting in buildings.

The standard weapon for these outings was a spring-powered BB gun. Air-powered BB guns had more power, but they took too long to load and pump to be suitable for this sort of rapid-fire action. Some preferred pellet guns, because lead pellets didn't ricochet the way copper BBs did, but pellets were more expensive than BBs.

A few killers even tried .22 birdshot, but this was mostly just a novelty. Although undeniably effective, birdshot shells were too expensive. They also frightened cattle and horses. This was serious, since farm owners were a little apprehensive anyway about carloads of FFA boys with guns around their sheds after dark.

Flashlights were great indicators of status. The serious

KNOCKIN' AROUND THE YARD

pest killer bought a six-volt lantern and carried an extra battery.

Quite a few birds were killed outside the sheds, making relatively easy targets perched on ledges or railings. Others, though, roosted inside the railings of shed doors, which on machine sheds had to be high enough to admit combines. It took good shooting to hit them through the crack in the railing. Then you needed a long stick to knock the birds out of the railing.

The most furious pest killing, however, went on inside the sheds, especially those that could be closed tight to trap roosting birds. Where there were openings that could not be closed, someone had to discourage the birds from exiting. This need gave rise to the greatest technological breakthrough in the history of pest contesting.

That was the tennis racket. The birds knew where the holes were, and they flew right past anyone trying to stop them, unless he had something to knock them down with. Tennis rackets were much more effective for this than were simple clubs, and they hurt less when you accidentally smacked your teammate instead of the bird flying between you. A good racket man could ascend to the top of the loft and close off the hay-rail opening, brandishing a flashlight in one hand and a tennis racket in the other and clinging to the ladder with his feet.

The grisly postscript to this affair was that the contestants had to present proof of their killings in the form of bird heads and animal tails. That accounts for those bulging FFA jacket pockets and those mysterious bags stowed in school lockers.—*TI*

23. *Knockin' Around the Yard*

WE have devoted quite a bit of space to the subject of agricultural pests—jackrabbits, starlings, grasshoppers, chinch bugs, and so on. Although some of this material may turn the stomachs of the uninitiated, it is nonetheless intriguing, because the odd battles man wages with pests tell us much about his relationship with the land.

This subject came up one winter afternoon in, of all places, the Faculty Club at the University of Calgary. I had just given a lecture on folk songs of the Great Plains to a folklore class, and the instructor, Tim Rodgers, took me to lunch with a gaggle of professors and associate deans and such people.

In that genteel company it was not I but Rodgers who brought up the subject of extermination of pests. Rodgers was president of the Canadian Folksong Society, and he wanted to tell me about a fine old song, "Knockin' Around the Yard." The subject of the song is a boy who spends his time "knockin' around the yard" with a stick, killing gophers for the bounty on their tails. This evidently was a common way for boys in Alberta and Saskatchewan to pick up some pocket change. Rodgers added that some boys were too softhearted to kill the creatures for their tails, and so they trapped the gophers alive, spun them around, wrung off their tails, and turned them loose again. This was called a "ring job."

So—I told him the story of FFA pest contests. By this time other diners at the table were starting their own conversations, but we were not be be stopped. I announced that as a boy I had bagged countless cottontail rabbits with no weapons other than a gunny sack and a croquet ball.

On the farm where I grew up in Barton County, Kansas, we had the home quarter under irrigation with gated pipe. The pipe were connected to the well pump with a line of straight four-inch aluminum pipe. There were always piles of four-inch pipe in the fields (all of our pipe were thirty feet long, incidentally, and I still can estimate distances accurately by visualizing how many irrigation pipe it would take to reach between two points).

Whenever one of our dogs chased up a rabbit, it would run into one of those pipe and think it was safe. Not so. While the dogs pranced about, barking and running from one end of the pipe to the other, I came up with a gunny sack and wrapped it around one end of the pipe. Then I walked to the other end, picked it up, dropped in the croquet ball, and raised the end of the pipe over my head. After some scratching and sliding around in the pipe, the rabbit would emerge into the gunny sack.

This method failed only when the dogs chased two or three rabbits into the same pipe. Then the rabbits would get together and hold back even three or four croquet balls.

An acceptable substitute for the croquet ball was a hedge apple, or Osage orange. A hedge apple wasn't perfectly round, but it was a little heavier than a croquet ball and sometimes even more effective.

It was a shame that some of the academicians at the table disdained this line of conversation, which we had pursued purely in the interest of scholarship. Some of them even acted as though I had made up the story. They probably believe in jackalopes, though.—*TI*

24. *Prairie Chickens*

NOVEMBER is prairie-chicken season, at least in the Flint Hills of Kansas. At one time prairie chickens of one sort or another could be found over nearly all of the country. The eastern variety, the heath hen, however, became extinct earlier in this century, and today only a few Atwater's prairie chickens survive along the Texas Gulf Coast.

The lesser prairie chicken, found primarily in the Texas and Oklahoma panhandles, northeastern New Mexico, southwestern Kansas, and southeastern Colorado, is a little better off, but the most populous subspecies is the greater prairie chicken. This bird ranges from the Midwest (Michigan and Indiana) to the Great Plains (Saskatchewan to Texas). It is well known for its colorful courtship ritual. The male inflates two bright-orange air sacs on his throat and makes a booming sound that can be heard for long distances across the prairies.

During earlier times on the plains prairie chickens were so numerous that they were a staple of the pioneer diet.

This abundance continued well into this century. As late as the 1920s, according to one old book lying around my house, the daily bag limit was fifty birds.

I do question the reliability of this anonymous authority, for he also states that prairie chickens are an inferior game bird, slow of wing and easily approached. Well, they must have gotten more wary in the past fifty years, because I know a lot of people who go home empty-handed after a day of chicken hunting.

About a dozen years back residents of my hometown put up a sign: "Cassoday, Prairie Chicken Capital of the World." The local Lions Club started sponsoring a hunt, selling permits and meals as a money-raising project and getting some national publicity in the process. That brought in the hunters, who thinned the bird population a bit, but there are still quite a few prairie chickens in the bluestem pastures there.

And they are good game birds. Some people try walking them out of the big pastures, but a chicken will often get up a quarter of a mile in front of the walkers. One of the best ways to hunt them is to know what milo or soybean fields they are used to feeding in of a morning, then hide out there and wait.

My father has an even better method, but it requires a field of shocked kaffir corn, and there just aren't many of those to be found these days. Dad has never been much of a hunter, but he did like a good prairie-chicken dinner once or twice a winter (this was back in the 1950s).

He would take the .22 along on the hayrack when he went out to get feed for the cows. If there were chickens in the field, some were sure to be feeding on the tops of the tipi-like shocks. Dad would tie up the mules and move toward the chickens, keeping a shock between himself and the birds until he got within range. More than once I have seen him shoot two birds off the same shock. The first one would often tumble over the others after it was shot, but prairie chickens aren't frightened by sound; they won't fly unless they see something that startles them.

I remember hearing of one carload of city hunters who

pulled into the Cassoday cafe, saying that they couldn't figure out why people thought prairie chickens were so hard
to shoot; they had gotten their limit in just a few minutes.
Then they opened the trunk of their car and proudly displayed a dozen meadowlarks.—*JH*

25.   *Turtle Races*

THE local youth program here sometimes sponsors a turtle
race for younger children during the summer. From what
I can ascertain, the kids provide their own turtles, the
prizes are things like free passes to the swimming pool, and
the whole enterprise seems to be devised to provide some
small measure of relief (for parent as well as child) from
the doldrums of summer vacation.

Fifty years past, however, turtle races, or terrapin der-
bies, as they were usually called, were a major diversion for
adults in the plains states. And the prizes were much more
substantial than a dip in the municipal pool. In 1930, for
instance, the 101 Ranch, of Ponca City, Oklahoma, was advertising a National Terrapin Derby, the seventh annual, to
be held in conjunction with its world-famous rodeo and
wild West show.

In that same year Floyd Sanford was promoting a major
professional rodeo in El Dorado, Kansas, and one of the
side attractions was a terrapin derby. Milt Hinkle, who
produced rodeos from Texas to Montana, wrote to Sanford from Dickinson, North Dakota, to find out how to run
a derby. Their letters provide a fascinating glimpse into
the world of big-time turtle racing.

Sanford had arranged for one thousand box tortoises
to be shipped in from Garden City, in the far-western part
of the state, paying ten cents a turtle. The race itself operated something like a lottery. Each turtle had a number
painted on its back, and people would "buy" a number
(with attached turtle) for two dollars. Several preliminary
heats were run, and the winners of these heats were pitted

against one another in a final dash for the dollars—three hundred dollars for the lucky "owner."

The track itself was a large chalk circle with twelve line judges spaced along the circumference. Turtles were kept in a large pan with no top or bottom, cables attached to lift it into the air at the starting gun. As a terrapin crossed the finish line, one of the line judges would hold it aloft, and the starter (who also served as the umpire) would note the order of the first five in each heat. These turtles were then put aside for the grand finale.

Total prize money to be awarded at El Dorado was estimated to be around $500, cost of the turtles $100. Income from the "sale" for the race was $2,000. Not a bad take, but that wasn't all. After the race was over, the turtles were to be sold for real—and at a cost of $1 each, a profit margin of 1,000 percent. No wonder rodeo promoters were in the turtle-racing business. Profits like those were better than collecting rain insurance on an indoor rodeo!

The Sanford and Hinkle rodeos, though, were merely the bush tracks of the turtle-racing circuit. At the top of the line, the 101 Ranch was expecting record-setting entries of thousands of turtles for its Seventh Annual National Terrapin Derby. A series of elimination heats would narrow this field to fifty, and of these the five fastest would collect the big money.

How big? I haven't seen the figures for 1930, but first prize for the 1929 derby was $6,580.—JH

26.   *Roping Bears*

A WHILE BACK I read a news story about two cowboys roping a bear in the Cimarron National Grassland near Elkhart, in the far southwest corner of Kansas. Apparently a black bear had strayed across the border from some forest land in Colorado and had to be roped and loaded into a stock trailer to be taken back.

Reading about the incident reminded me of the natural

cowboy tendency to try to rope anything he sees. Vaqueros
in Spanish California roped grizzly bears regularly, as did
cowboys in Montana, if Charlie Russell's paintings are at all
indicative. Many old-time rodeo cowboys have told me that
they learned to rope by catching everything that moved on
the family farm: dogs, goats, pigs—even chickens.

Roping coyotes is not uncommon on the plains, and it's
something I always wanted to do when I was younger. Unfortunately (or maybe not) I never got close enough to
even throw at one. I did try roping a badger once, but it
was too low to the ground and could jump backwards too
quickly for me to catch. Bert Plummer, one of the old
settlers at my hometown, Cassoday, in the Kansas Flint
Hills, did once catch a jackrabbit, my father told me. Bert
was getting the milk cows in on their kid horse, riding
bareback with a halter. The halter rope was extralong, so
he had tied a honda in one end and was passing the time
by roping weeds. The rabbit catch, famous in local annals,
was a fluke, a long throw at a sitting rabbit, the loop just
barely fitting over its head as it leaped up to run.

Another story the bear-roping reminded me of was one
I heard over twenty years ago when I was working for the
Flying A, a company producing a rodeo in McCook, Nebraska. The story may be apocryphal, but it should have
happened even if it didn't.

It seems that a filling-station owner in western Nebraska
had a small menagerie to help attract custom: some raccoons, a couple of mangy coyotes, and—the prize attraction—a bear. But the bear died (whether from age, mal-
nutrition, or gasoline fumes I don't know).

One day the owner was sitting around drinking beer
with a buddy and lamenting his loss when he got a bright
idea: they would go to Yellowstone and get another bear.
So he loaded two coolers (one with beer and one with hamburger patties), and the two fellows headed for Wyoming.

When they got there, all went according to plan. They
parked the old Chevy in bear country, opened the trunk,
put the spare tire in the back seat, laid a trail of hamburger, and sat back to drink some beer and wait. Before

long they had a bear eating his way into their trap. Once he was in the trunk, they slammed the lid on him and headed for home.

They almost made it there before disaster struck. First they ran out of beer, and then they blew a tire. The spare was in the back seat, but the jack was still in the trunk! Things got even worse when a highway patrolman pulled up to offer some help.

The filling-station man and his friend were, understandably, nervous when the patrolman asked them to open the trunk; the trooper grew, understandably, suspicious when they refused to open it. In this predrug era, he thought they were murderers transporting a body. So he pulled his gun on them and radioed for backup. By the time help arrived, the culprits had decided that poaching was a lesser crime than suspicion of murder and confessed, but their story was so preposterous that the troopers didn't believe them. Nevertheless, they opened the trunk with extreme care.

The bear, hamburger long since exhausted, was not happy in his small, stuffy quarters, and the patrolmen had one heck of a time getting the lid reclosed. When they did, they were more than ready to throw the book at the two poachers. But park rangers, when contacted, said that if the bear was returned they would not press charges.

So the tire was changed, and the bear thieves began their long, dry drive back to Yellowstone, accompanied by a Nebraska highway-patrol escort. At the state line the Wyoming highway patrol was waiting to continue the escort, all the way to Yellowstone.—*JH*

27. *The Official Great Plains Animal*

IF you were to choose an animal that best represents the spirit of the plains, what would it be? If the choice were a bird, I doubt if there would be much question; five of the

Great Plains states (Kansas, Nebraska, Wyoming, North Dakota, and Montana) have already named the western meadowlark—bright and sunny with the sweetest song this side of Keats's nightingale—as their state bird.

But if it were a mammal, which would it be? I don't know how many of the plains states have named an official animal, but I have a feeling that many of them would do what Kansas has already done, choose the American bison.

There is no doubt that in the popular mind the buffalo represents the Great Plains—it is associated with the Plains Indians, with the building of the railroads (William F. Cody got his nickname by killing bison to feed railroad workers), with the hide hunters in the Great Slaughter, and with the overwhelming sense of space evoked by the Great Plains (travel narratives tell of moving for days through seemingly endless herds of bison).

The bison is majestic and noble in appearance, was important historically, and has a powerful emotional appeal, evoking mythically (if somewhat nostalgically) our last frontier. These same attributes could be used in making a case for naming either the mustang or the Texas longhorn as the official animal of the Great Plains. Both of these are originally domesticated animals that achieved freedom on the plains and then, like the bison, were nearly exterminated before efforts were made to save them. Today all three animals are safe from extinction, but probably none of them will ever again enjoy the numbers—or the freedom—that they once knew.

My own choice for official Great Plains animal, however, roams just as freely today as it ever did, and in undiminished numbers. It has been hunted with hounds, with clubs, with guns, with horses, with automobiles, with airplanes, with radios. It has been sought for its fur and for its ears (bounty money). It has been cursed, falsely accused of the crimes of others, and maligned for its supposed sneakiness and cowardice. But it has survived.

The coyote.

The coyote has been here every bit as long as the bison

and much longer than the longhorn or the mustang. Plains Indians revered the coyote (and used it in developing their own domesticated dogs), and each tribe had its own version of a coyote deity, a trickster that helped teach humankind the art of survival.

There's no question that coyotes eat chickens, and, as an old-time cowboy (and sheep-hater) from Idaho once told me, "Sheep meat won't hurt a coyote." But I really think that dogs are probably responsible for killing most of the calves that coyotes get caught eating. That controversy is an emotional one (and I'd be happy to hear from readers who have opinions), but I've yet to be convinced that coyotes are a major threat to the cattlemen.

The coyote, like the Great Plains itself, has adapted to and prospered from change and adversity, retaining its essential nature throughout. The bison, the longhorn, and the mustang are all behind fences now, but the coyote still represents the freedom—and the challenge—of life on the plains.—*JH*

Part Three

HORSE AND CATTLE CULTURE

BOTH Tom and I have often noted that the folk method of doing something or other can be just as effective as the latest scientific method. The same tenet holds true for animals; the old-fashioned are sometimes the most up to date. For instance, the most popular and useful breed of horse in the plains today, the quarter horse, wasn't even recognized as a breed until 1939, even though the type was around at least as early as the Revolutionary War.

An even better example is the Texas longhorn, the legendary bovine that filled the Kansas and Nebraska cowtowns from the late 1860s until tamer, meatier British breeds replaced them. At one time the longhorn almost followed the bison into extinction, but fortunately a few head were placed, along with deer, elk, and bison, on the Wichita Wildlife Refuge, near Cache, Oklahoma.

Then, in 1964, Charlie Schreiner, of Mountain Home, Texas, started the Texas Longhorn Breeders Association of America. Schreiner had been attending the annual auction of surplus animals at the Wichita Wildlife Refuge for nine years. Along with a few other dedicated breeders—fellow Texans Cap Yates and M. P. Wright, Jr., and Harry Pon, of Burns, Oregon, among others—he had been building up a herd of longhorns, and he thought it was time to attempt to give the breed official status, as well as to make it more commercially viable.

Longhorns weren't worth much back in those days. In fact, they were considered "zoo cattle," curiosities to be kept around the ranch as pets and living reminders of the Old West. At weaning age a longhorn calf would bring maybe a hundred dollars, while an aged steer with a nice set of horns brought only three times that.

The people who started the TLBAA, most of whom had been handling Texas longhorns for several years, recognized that these cattle had traits that should be worth something in the marketplace. This was the time of the exotics, of Charolais, Limousin, and Simmental, so why not the Texas longhorn? Today $100,000 bulls and $30,000 cows are not uncommon. At one longhorn production sale in Texas last year, for instance, cattle sold for an average of over $10,000 a head.

The desirable longhorn traits include a high fertility rate and a mother cow that will produce calves for years and years. When a longhorn goes off to have a calf, another cow goes along with her to stand guard against predators. More important to many ranchers is the size of the calf dropped by a first-calf Angus or Hereford heifer when crossed with a longhorn bull. The calves are so small that birthing difficulties with longhorns are almost unheard of. Not only that, but the wiry little calf will be on its feet and ready to run much more quickly than calves of other breeds.

In short, longhorns, having lived for centuries under survival-of-the-fittest conditions, are extremely hardy. Like the buffalo, they can survive, even thrive, on range that appears to be nothing but brush and sand. Their meat, in this age of cholesterol consciousness, is lean, but not tough and stringy.

In case this begins to sound like an advertisement, let me hasten to say that I don't own a single Texas longhorn (although I do have a nice set of six-foot horns hanging in my office). I'm just impressed with the comeback made by these fascinating plains animals.—*JH*

29. *More on Longhorns*

BECAUSE of my interest in the Texas longhorn, I have written some magazine articles about contemporary Kansas breeders of Texas longhorns (Dick Robbins, of Pratt, and Dick Pringle, of Yates Center). These articles resulted in an invitation to attend the 1984 meeting of the Texas Longhorn Breeders Association of America held in Amarillo. There I learned that some twenty-three hundred members of the TLBAA own over 72,000 registered Texas long-horns. Quite a contrast to the thirty-seven charter members of 1964. In August of that year only 104 cattle were on the registry.

One problem faced in the early years of the association was deciding just what sort of breed guidelines should be established. Even Charlie Schreiner (who organized the association) could get only sixty-seven of the nearly one hundred head of longhorns on his Y O Ranch accepted. The first TLBAA field inspector was Claude ("Heck") Schrader, who had spent much of his working life on the Wichita Wildlife Refuge, where the longhorn was, many people believe, saved from extinction.

And what are the characteristics of the breed? I've mentioned some of them earlier—easy calving, general hardiness. But first of all, you have to have horns. A standard color doesn't matter; longhorns come in all sorts of colors. A longhorn (steer or cow) should be straight-backed and not too hefty-looking. The cows tend to be of lighter weight than cows of the British breeds. In fact, a Hereford man would probably think that a prize-winning longhorn cow looked rangy and hungry.

The origins of the Texas longhorn are lost, as the cliché goes, in the mists of antiquity. Wild aurochs from northern Europe and Moorish cattle from Africa came together in Spain sometime around the tenth century, providing the basis of the Andalusian cattle that were first brought to the New World in 1494. The cattle industry was well established by the time Coronado began his explorations into the southern and central plains in 1540, bringing with him some five hundred head of cattle.

The strays from this herd (and from cattle escaping from the Texas missions and presidios established in the seventeenth and eighteenth centuries) were well suited to (and well served by) the rich grasses of the plains, multiplying rapidly. By the time Texas became a state, there were plenty of "criollo"—cattle of the country—throughout Mexico and the Southwest.

During the nineteenth century these criollo cattle came into contact with cattle from the eastern and southern United States (known as Native American cattle) and with the Zebu, introduced from India around the time of the Civil War. From these influences came the Texas longhorn of the trail-driving days.

Texas longhorns had a reputation for meanness, even ferocity, in the old days. Modern breeders claim that the reputation was exaggerated, that today's longhorns, while independent and self-reliant, can be gentle if handled right. But, as Dick Robbins told me when I was photographing his herd, "Don't ever step between a longhorn cow and her calf."—*JH*

30. *Wild Cow Milking*

WILD COW MILKING is a crowd-pleasing rodeo event usually found today only at smaller local shows, but it was once a major part of big-time professional rodeo in the United States and is still popular in Canadian rodeo. In the late 1930s and early 1940s, in fact, world championships were given, according to Bud Shutts, of Beaumont, Kansas, who once came close to winning the title.

This event is closely related to actual ranch work, for many times a range cow with a newborn calf has to be roped and milked out if her baby cannot take all of her milk. That's definitely not the sort of job one wants to take on without some help!

According to the usual rodeo rules, two cowboys on horseback chase a cow. One ropes her and dallies the loose end of the rope around the saddle horn while his partner, the mugger, jumps off his horse and attempts to hold the cow while the roper squirts a bit of milk into a pop bottle, then runs back to the starting line. The cow, however, is almost never cooperative, which makes things rough on cowboys and great entertainment for crowds.

I remember one rodeo I went to in Missouri several years ago that had some rather unusual rules. Teams were composed of three unmounted men, and everybody was in the arena at the same time. Then a bunch of Brahma cows were turned loose. At first the cowboys chased after the cows, but after about two passes through the muddy arena, the cows got hot—and mad. From then on things began to look like a bullfight, with ropes instead of capes, as the cowboys tried to dodge a cow and drop a rope around her neck as she went past.

I wasn't entered in that particular cow milking, but I was, unfortunately, at another rodeo where the cow left the chute with a rope around her neck, the other end in the cowboy's hand. In this case I was mugging for a couple of younger boys who were entering their first rodeo. With the roping aspect guaranteed, of course, the crowd got to see more muggers in action, which was the main point as far as the rodeo promoter was concerned. But for me it was a different story. The day was hot, and the cows were uncooperative. We got through the first run reasonably well, but, as I recall, the second boy didn't even get a chance to do any milking.

One of the most frustrating aspects of wild cow milking is when the roper ropes, the mugger mugs—but the cow is dry. At an El Dorado, Kansas, rodeo around 1930, one former contestant told me, about twenty-five teams were entered in the cow milking. Instead of running one team at a time, twenty-five cows were turned into the area at once, with fifty mounted cowboys at the far end. At a signal, mass mayhem broke loose as ropers charged cows. My informant remembers that there was only one dry cow in the bunch and that it was roped by Merle Teter. Teter, one of the most prominent cattlemen in that part of the state, took quite a ribbing from his fellow competitors for not being able to tell a milker from a dry cow—even on the run.

Roping cows calls for a different kind of loop from that used in either calf or steer roping—a kind of sidearm throw that rolls the rope around and over the cow's head.

One of the masters of this kind of roping is Bob Alexander, who has run cattle in the Flint Hills near Council Grove for many years. I also remember watching my uncle, Marshall Hoy, roll a loop on cows at Countryman's rodeo, near Cassoday. In fact, more than one person has told me that Marshall and Wilbur Countryman were the cow-milking team to beat in their day. Both were good ropers, both rode fast horses, and Wilbur was left-handed, so whichever way the cow jumped after she left the chute, one of them was ready to pop a loop on her.

The Winfield, Kansas, rodeo sponsors a businessmen's cow milking each year, a real crowd pleaser. Cows held on ropes by mounted cowboys are turned loose for teams of local businessmen to try to milk. If it's fun to watch cowboys get dragged and stomped by angry cows, it's hilarious to see it happen to your banker, your grocer, or your insurance man.

Wild cow milking is the demolition derby of rodeo— lots of excitement and wrecks, but rarely any serious injuries.—*JH*

31. *Bone Pickers*

ONE thing that has surprised me in my observation of Great Plains folk life is how much of what we ordinarily think of as pioneer custom actually carried over well into the twentieth century. Such things as pasturing cattle on open range and homesteading in dugouts were taking place in western Kansas in the late 1920s—and in the Texas and Oklahoma panhandles and other areas of the plains as well. Not long ago I read (in Stan Steiner's *The Ranchers*) of people traveling in covered wagons from central Texas into New Mexico during the Great Depression; they had lost not only their farms but their Model Ts as well.

Recently I learned of another example of a pioneer activity—bone picking—that occurred at least once in the post–World War I period. Bone picking was a reasonably lucrative, if monotonous, occupation in the 1870s and 1880s, just after the great bison slaughter. Ordinary bones brought around eight dollars a ton delivered to a railhead, hooves and horns almost twice that. According to David Dary's thorough and entertaining *Buffalo Book,* 16,000 tons of bones were shipped east between 1872 and 1874, over 5,000 tons on the Santa Fe alone. One stack, awaiting shipment at Granada, Colorado, was twelve feet high, twelve feet wide—and half a mile long!

Bone gathering was done both by professional pickers and by homesteading families that were in need of some quick cash. Often a farmer turned to bone picking after grasshoppers had dropped in for some corn or wheat picking, but sometimes the farmer had to pick bones even before he could get a plow into the earth. One old drawing shows a sodbuster plowing his first furrow, the area on one side newly cleared of bones, the rest of the prairie literally covered with them.

Grandpa Gooch, my mother's maternal grandfather, got his start in life by picking bones in Oklahoma and hauling them to Wichita during the mid-1870s. He had come to Sumner County, Kansas, as a young man, too late to hunt buffalo, but he took advantage of the aftermath of the slaughter by earning enough money to set himself up in the corn market.

But all of this is merely background to the real subject of this chapter—bone picking in the 1920s. My father tells me that early one summer an older man drove into Cassoday, Kansas, in a light wagon drawn by a single horse. He spent all that summer in the big pastures surrounding the town, hauling bleached steer bones to the railroad siding near the Cassoday depot. Dad doesn't remember the exact year, but it was not long after the railroad came to town in 1923.

Cassoday is in the middle of the Flint Hills, where Texas steers have been part of the landscape since the days of the

Chisholm Trail. There were no nearby desiccating companies in those days, and the aged steers shipped into the bluestem pastures each spring came in from Texas thin and
weak. Within a few months most of them would have gained
hundreds of pounds, but some died in the early weeks, especially if April had been cold and wet. Others would have
succumbed to blackleg or screwworms, or have been struck
by lightning. Cattle have been summer-pastured in this
area since the 1850s, so the Cassoday bone picker had
plenty of bones to gather. By the end of the summer he
had put together a big pile, enough to fill an entire railroad car.

What happened to him then no one knows. Maybe the
next season he followed the Flint Hills north into Morris or
Wabaunsee County; maybe he moved south into the Osage
region of Oklahoma. There were not many range areas
left at that time that had the right conditions to provide
large numbers of bones.

Were there others like him, old men carrying on a trade
they had perhaps learned as teenagers on the frontier? I
wish I knew.—*JH*

32. *Rodeo Stunts*

Now that rodeo is trying its best to emulate other professional sports, and cattle work is becoming more and more
mechanized, the wild and crazy stunts that once could be
seen in range country or at rodeos are rapidly fading from
memory.

One of my favorite stories is about a black cowboy from
the Texas Panhandle, Bones Hooks, who, with the passing
of the open range, had become a porter on the Santa Fe
Railroad. His reputation as a rider was such, however, that
when he heard about a generous prize for riding a tough
bronc in Pampa, he arranged for the horse to be waiting
and for the engineer to stop the train long enough to allow
him to strap on a pair of borrowed spurs, ride the outlaw

down the city streets, and send a telegram to the next station: "Horse rode, money collected, train on time."

Another early-day Texas bronc rider was the famous "Booger Red" Privett. Booger Red, like Bill Pickett (the black cowboy of the 101 Ranch who invented bulldogging), has attained almost legendary status. More than one cowboy affected the name, but the real Booger Red was both a rodeo cowboy and the proprietor of a "bronc show," an exhibition of bucking horses that operated as a sideshow at carnivals. He got his nickname from the vivid reddish-colored scars on his face, the result of a childhood firecracker accident.

Booger Red was nothing if not sure of himself. He would do things like ride a saddle bronc with both hands waving freely in the air—or with both of them securely tied behind him. On two separate—and documented—occasions he rode a bronc while holding his own baby in his free arm. What he lacked in common sense he more than made up for in confidence!

One of the most impossible-sounding stunts I ever heard of was undertaken by Fred Pickering, of Herington, Kansas, at the 1915 Burdick Field Day rodeo. According to the reporter of the *Council Grove Republican,* Pickering rode "a large vicious mule cleanly and consistently both ways." What the reporter meant by "both ways" is that, after bucking him out in a normal fashion, Pickering placed the saddle backward on the mule and rode, without using either hand, while facing the animal's tail. I have a photograph showing the rearward-facing saddle, the rider making final adjustments just before being turned loose. Unfortunately, I do not have a picture of the ride itself, nor can I even imagine, despite the bronc riding I did in my earlier years, what the ride must have been like.

Another episode wasn't actually a stunt; it was a contest ride—but the rider, a woman named Mattie Downs, was over eight months pregnant at the time. Her baby (full term, by the way) was born seventeen days later. The informant who gave me the photograph said that Mattie rode the horse to a standstill because she didn't want to get thrown off and hurt (I wasn't told why she got on the horse in the first place). I don't know much else about Mattie, except that the bronc ride was probably at a 1930s rodeo in Olpe or Eureka, Kansas, that Mattie was probably from either Chase or Greenwood county, and that her husband's name was Bobby. Personally, I think she should have been married to Booger Red.—*JH*

33. *More Rodeo Stunts*

THE previous chapter tells about some of the wild and crazy stunts that took place at early-day rodeos, including an account of Fred Pickering, who rode a bucking mule backward. I have since learned of several other cowboys who rode broncs backward, but I think all of them were upstaged by Jack Redcloud, who once tried to bulldog a steer from an airplane.

While you're coming to grips with that bit of idiocy, let me fill you in on some of the other rodeo stunts I have learned about. Earlier in this century steer riders often added some spectacle to their contests by fastening a bell to a strap around the animal's neck (instead of having it attached to the riding rope, as occurs today), then attempting to unbuckle the strap while riding. Frank Frey, of Strong City, Kansas, tried that event at the Burdick rodeo in the late teens but couldn't get the bell off. On the other hand, Marion Beougher, of Gove, Kansas, got so good at it that he was asked not to compete at the Oakley rodeo so that other people could have a chance to win.

Another common steer- or cow-riding ploy, often performed when the arena director thought the crowd needed an attention getter, was to have double riders. I have photographs from several early-day rodeos that show one cowboy riding in the usual position with a rope or surcingle while a second cowboy (or rodeo clown) has straddled the animal's neck and is facing backward.

Rodeo clowns would also do things like strap a washtub or a rocking chair onto the back of a steer or bronc, then climb aboard for a crowd-thrilling trip. Usually a short one.

Ordinary steer wrestling itself was definitely a spectacle back in the days before the outlawing of the houlihan, whereby a steer was flipped by sticking one of his horns into the ground on the dead run, rather than pulling him to a stop and twisting him down. Apparently, however, that wasn't enough for Dick Truitt at the Sun City rodeo in the late 1930s. I have a couple of photographs showing Truitt bulldogging a fullgrown bison. Rodeo producer Marion McLain had promised Truitt twenty dollars if he got the buffalo thrown, nothing for just trying. Truitt collected.

The McLain Stampede was the site of the airplane bull-dogger promised earlier. I have photographs of both men and women bulldogging from automobile running boards, but that was mere child's play to Jack Redcloud. He was not a cowboy but a daredevil of some sort who earlier in the day (this was around 1935) had done some wing walking with a barnstorming pilot. His bulldogging stunt involved hanging from a rope ladder on a low-flying, slow-flying plane, then trying to land on a steer being hazed by several cowboys down the long arena on the McLain ranch. He missed.

The dust cloud, Bud Shutts told me, was maybe not the largest ever in Barber County, but it was a big one. Redcloud wasn't hurt seriously in the mishap, but the results of his next stunt, later that evening, were not so fortunate. The last thing Max McLain remembers of Redcloud is his being taken to the hospital for some stomach pumping; he had passed the hat, then eaten an assortment of razor blades and carpet tacks for the assembled spectators.—*JH*

34. *Bulldogging*

Iᴛ's always a thrill when a local boy makes good, so I was really happy to see Joel Edmonson, of Columbus, Kansas, become the World's Champion steer wrestler for 1983. Joel was a one-man rodeo team here at Emporia State University in the mid-1970s, riding barebacks and dogging steers.

Bulldoggers have a reputation for being pretty tough. According to one bit of lore I have heard, this is the standard test for aspiring bulldoggers: Get somebody to drive you down a dirt road at about thirty-five miles per hour, then open the car door and look down. If you can jump, you can be a bulldogger. Actually, steer wrestling, as it is officially called today, is not quite that hazardous; jumping from a horse onto a running steer, stopping him, and twisting him down by the horns requires nerve, but not as much as diving out of a moving car.

Still, as with the forward pass in football, a lot can go wrong, and only one thing can go right. The steer can set up, and the dogger will go flying out into the dirt in front of him. The dogging horse can slow up, and the dogger will go tumbling into the dirt behind the steer. Or the dogging horse can crowd into the steer, throwing the dogger under the hooves of the hazer's horse. Among other things.

Bulldogging today, though, is not as dangerous as it was in the early part of this century. Then the steers tended to be bigger (eight hundred to one thousand pounds as opposed to five hundred to seven hundred pounds today) and fresh out of the pasture. I have several pictures of bulldoggers in the 1920s pulling on one horn with their arms while their legs are wrapped in a wrestling hold around the nose and the other horn. It took a lot of twisting to bring down some of those rubber-necked steers.

Sometimes, if horned steers were not available, rodeo producers back then would use cows. The producer would certainly get his money's worth: using the calves for roping and their mothers for wild cow milking, cow riding, and bulldogging (cowdogging?). Some of those cows never could be twisted down.

For a little extra excitement some rodeo producers would stage a buffalo bulldogging. In my collection of early rodeo photographs are two of Dick Truitt, famous

roper of the 1930s, bulldogging a full-grown bison at the
McLain Stampede in the Gypsum Hills of Kansas. The first
picture shows him sliding down onto the buffalo from his
running horse (Bob Crosby is the hazer); the second shows
the buffalo flat on the ground, Truitt dusty and grimacing.

At Kiowa, Kansas, around 1928 a man slipped down
into the bucking chute with a full-grown bison, grabbed his
horns, and was turned into the arena, where he spent the
next fifteen or twenty minutes trying to wrestle the brute
to the ground. Meanwhile, I am told, roping and riding
events continued around the struggling pair. The man, by
the way, won the contest.

Back in the teens they used to bulldog by houlihaning.
That is, the dogger would jump onto the running steer's
head (instead of starting just back of the shoulders as modern doggers do) and try to stick one of the horns into the
ground. If he was successful, the steer would be flipped
over with a thud. It would also often break a horn or a neck,
which is one reason that this practice was soon outlawed.

The other reason is that the steer would also sometimes
come down on top of the cowboy. Jerry Wright was killed
at the 1921 Parsons, Kansas, rodeo in just this fashion. Fortunately today's rules make bulldogging a safer sport for
both man and steer.

How did bulldogging originate? That's another story.
—JH

35. *Bill Pickett and the Origin of Bulldogging*

AS PROMISED EARLIER, I'm going to take another look at
the cowboy sport of bulldogging. I suppose that, techni-
cally speaking, the world's first bulldogging occurred when
Theseus tamed the minotaur in the Labyrinth of ancient
Crete. There is also a traditional Chinese folk sport in which
men on foot wrestle horned oxen to the ground.

As far as American rodeo is concerned, bulldogging

began around the turn of the century with a black Texas cowboy named Bill Pickett. Pickett, born in 1870 or 1871, spent most of his adult life with the 101 Ranch, of Ponca City, Oklahoma, riding its pastures and performing in its world-famous wild West show.

Pickett was an excellent roper and bronc and steer rider, but his most acclaimed feat was bulldogging. He would leap from his horse onto a running steer, pull it to a stop, tip its head up, sink his teeth into its lip, then throw his hands into the air and fall over backward, pulling the steer to the ground in the process. This stunt was so spectacular that it soon gained legendary status. True to the folk process, even eyewitnesses saw more than had actually occurred.

Here is what one elderly man (then a small boy) remembers seeing at the Burdick, Kansas, Field Day rodeo in 1915:

"He rode into town from the southeast on a little Indian pony, the first black man I'd ever seen. He rode right up to a group of cowboys and told them that if they'd loan him a fast horse he'd show them something they had never seen before. Then he got on E. T. Anderson's big steer-roping horse, cut out a longhorn, and gave chase. When he got up to the steer, he dove off the horse, slid headfirst between the horns, and as he went past he bit the steer's lip, turned a somersault, and landed on his feet flipping the steer down with a thud!"

A similar account was published in a Tulsa newspaper just months before Pickett died in 1932:

"Coming up on the steer's near side, the rider leaped from the saddle. He turned a complete somersault along the length of the steer's back, flying out and down over the curved horns to fasten his teeth in the side of the steer's mouth. With sheer strength he dragged the running behemoth's head to the tanbark, thrust its horns in the ground, and forward momentum threw the steer hocks over horns in a somersault of its own."

The writer goes on to say that Pickett did all of this without using his hands.

These two methods, it seems obvious to me, are physically impossible, but I do not think that either source was deliberately exaggerating. Rather, the man from Burdick was recalling a boyhood memory from some seventy years past, while the author of the newspaper article was writing not as an eyewitness but about stories told in retrospect. It also seems obvious to me that Bill Pickett has become a folk hero and that his exploits have taken on legendary status.

The best two surviving photographs of Pickett in action were taken at the Burdick Field Day. In one, Pickett quite clearly is biting the steer's lip and is leaning backward, his hand high in the air. In the second, the steer, an eight-hundred-pounder at least, is flat on the ground, and so is Pickett, teeth still firmly clamped.

Pickett is said to have bulldogged over five thousand steers in his lifetime; he is known to have lost all of his front teeth.—*JH*

36. *Selling Wild Horses*

AMONG the many writings of American Nobel Laureate William Faulkner are two versions of a story entitled "Spotted Horses." Both deal humorously with the exploits of Flem Snopes as he cons gullible Mississippi dirt farmers into buying some wild Texas horses. Once the new owners step into the corral to claim their purchases, the supposed "gentle but spirited" ponies turn out to be kickers and biters that tear the fence down and run away.

There are some horse sales, though, where no question exists about the nature of the animals: they are advertised as broncs, and the harder they buck, the higher the price. Miles City, Montana, for instance, holds a bucking-horse auction each year. The chute gate opens on a bareback or saddle bronc, and the bidding begins as soon as the rider is thrown, or the whistle is blown.

I remember a couple of bronc sales sponsored by the Roberts family, of Strong City, Kansas. Ken and Gerald

Roberts were both World's Champion rodeo cowboys (bull-riding and all-around, respectively), and Ken and his father, E. C., provided stock for rodeos all over the country in the 1940s and 1950s. The earlier sale was of some South Dakota horses, located and rounded up on Indian reservations there by Casey Tibbs.

The second auction was a sad day for me—it marked the dispersal of the Roberts string of bucking horses and bulls. It was held in an indoor arena in Salina during the winter of 1962. I remember that Jesse James, named "Bucking Horse of the Year" by professional saddle-bronc riders the next season, sold for over two thousand uninflated dollars. E. C. Roberts told me recently that they could have gotten many times that price if Jesse had won the title just a few months earlier.

In an earlier era of rodeo, sales of bucking horses were sometimes handled in a different fashion. Marion McLain, for instance, produced a rodeo in El Dorado, Kansas, in 1929, with some new broncs from wild-horse herds in Colorado. The ones that did a good job of bucking, he kept for future rodeos. The ones that didn't, he sold to Flint Hills ranchers.

Frank Cannon, of Rosalia, bought nine of them, his son Cliff told me, and parceled them out to be broken by local cowboys (two of these horsebreakers, I learned, were my father and my uncle). Cliff told me that these erstwhile mustangs might not have been good enough for a rodeo string, but they were good buckers nonetheless. He himself not only learned to ride saddle broncs on these "using" horses, but one horse in particular, used nearly daily for nine years as a cow horse, would still buck a rider off every chance he got.

During the 1920s, White Cloud's Rodeo (named after an Iowa chief) was held on the Iowa, Sac, and Fox Reservation in Doniphan County, Kansas. The practice there each year was to bring in wild horses from the western ranges, then to sell them to local farmers after the rodeo.

Alfred Zimmerman, of Troy, Kansas, remembers well

one of these broncs purchased by his father. "He would tremble and snort and jump around every time he was run into the barn, but once you threw a strap or rope of any kind over his shoulders, he would stand perfectly still to be harnessed. I guess he thought, when he felt that strap, that he had been roped and he might as well quit struggling."

The Kansas farmers and ranchers had two distinct advantages over the poor, duped sharecroppers of Faulkner's story—first, they knew exactly what kind of horses they were getting, and second, they knew how to handle them.—*JH*

37. *Horse Auctions*

HORSE AUCTIONS are variable affairs. They can range from fur-coat-and-champagne offerings of top-quality thoroughbreds to levis-and-cheap-bourbon-in-a-paper-sack consignments of anything on four legs at the local sale barn.

People tell me that the fancy sales are entertaining and impressive. I wouldn't know; I haven't gone to many purebred sales since an auctioneer friend knocked off a $20,000 Charolais bull to me a few years ago. He had lost his last live bid, and he needed to name a buyer so that the bull could be brought back into the ring later and resold. Even though I consciously realized all of this, that didn't keep my subconscious from tossing my heart into my throat when the gavel fell and I heard that I was the buyer.

Personally, I enjoy the backwoods (or back-prairie, to be more precise) horse sales, the ones where local farmers and ranchers bring their horses to sell alongside those of the few horse traders still roaming the countryside. Buying a horse at one of these sales is a test not only of one's judgment of horseflesh, but also of one's current standing with Dame Fortune. Sometimes you can pick up a real bargain; sometimes you just get someone else's problems.

I especially remember one young bay quarter-horse

gelding my father bought for two hundred dollars at an auction. He was registered, well built, easy to catch, and handled nicely, except for one thing—he was a bit light on his front feet. He liked to "rare over backwards," as we say in the Flint Hills.

The horse was passed along to me for some schooling, but I was never able to get him over this bad habit, so I unloaded him onto a horse trader for the two hundred dollars Dad had paid. Nothing for our feed, gasoline, or time—or the trauma of being an unwilling participant in the backflips of an eleven-hundred-pound animal.

The trader kept him for a while, paid to have him shod, and almost had him sold a few times. Those deals always fell through when the prospective buyer took a test ride— a very exciting ride.

A few months later I saw the bay horse in a sale ring. He still looked great, and he handled well. He should have; he had just come from a week's workout with a high-dollar horse trainer. That was the only way, the trader told me later that evening, that he could get the horse sold. The sale price? Two hundred dollars.—*JH*

38.   *Loading Horses*

ONE advantage the old-time cowboys had over us moderns was that they didn't have any horse trailers. Think about it—without horse trailers they didn't have to face the agonizing frustration of trying to load a horse that just wouldn't be loaded. I think that St. Francis himself might have become an animal hater if he had ever tried to push an obstinate horse into a trailer.

I have seen cattle that have been roped right out in the middle of an eight-section pasture literally run into a stock trailer when led near it. Then we have spent the next ten minutes trying to get one of the horses loaded in with the cattle.

Once trained, most horses will walk right into a trailer,

but getting them trained can be a problem. I have heard of all kinds of folk methods for teaching horses to load. Of these, pain is the least effective; if a horse is afraid of walking into a trailer, beating him only makes him more afraid.

One of the best methods with smaller horses is for two people to link hands, place their arms about midway down his tail, and with someone pulling on the halter rope, literally lift and shove him into the trailer.

Bigger horses can be more of a problem. Often a rope tied to one side of the trailer then passed around the back end of the horse and looped through the other side is effective. One person leads the horse into the trailer, another tightens the rope.

Even this trick doesn't always work, but my Uncle Marshall, who has been working with horses for some three-quarters of a century, taught me one that does. Get the horse up against the barn or a solid wall, put a couple of panels along either side of him, then back the trailer right under him. There's no place for the horse to go but into the trailer.

The best method of all is to load a colt a number of times with its mother or, if it's an older horse, feed it in the trailer, gradually setting the feed bucket closer toward the front until the horse has to get inside to get to it. Both methods acclimate the horse to the trailer without traumatizing him.

One of my favorite horse-trailering stories is not about loading, but about unloading. A cowboy from the Gypsum Hills of Kansas had a horse that was nearly perfect—the right size, a pretty color, well built, easy to catch, easy to load, good with cattle. He had just one thing wrong with him. No sooner was the trailer gate unlatched than that horse would come flying out. If anyone was in the way, too bad.

One day his owner was unloading him in a pasture to check some cattle and the horse charged out backward so fast that he knocked the cowboy stemwinding. He was so mad that he ran the horse back into the trailer—saddle, bridle, and all—and backed up to a pond dam. The pond

was about four or five feet deep at that spot, with about a
four-foot drop to the water itself. He just threw the gate
open and waited for the splash.

After that he had a nearly perfect horse—easy to catch,
well made, easy to load, good around cattle. He had just
one flaw. He was the hardest horse you ever saw to get out
of a trailer.—*JH*

39.   *Hotshots*

THE OTHER DAY, while pushing some calves along a chute
and wishing for a hotshot, I began thinking about the
many different types of cattle prods that I had seen over
the years. In some parts of the West, stockmen carried bull-
whips to use when moving cattle. This use was rare in my
part of the plains. We used sticks or buggy whips while
working cattle on foot, a rope if on horseback.

Until the late 1950s, most of the cattle shipped into or
out of the Cassoday–Matfield Green region of the Kansas
Flint Hills moved by train. Mounted cowboys in the pens
would sometimes use the end of a lariat rope, or perhaps a
sunflower they had pulled up, as a whip; those along the
loading ramps used sticks or canes. Some of us kids would
occasionally swing from a gate bar out over the loading
cattle and rake the slower ones with our spurs.

Commission men and cattle buyers usually carried canes
or special prod poles about six feet long, especially when
they were on their home turf—the stockyards. I can still
smell the cigars and see the spittoons and the canes in the
Livestock Commission Building at Wichita (I remember
vividly the man with a bull-pizzle cane!). On my first trip to
the Kansas City yards (I think I was about ten or twelve
years old), I was allowed to buy a cane for a souvenir. I
never could bring myself to use it on cattle and get it dirty.

The first electric cattle prods (which we always called
hotshots—I wonder what other names they go by?) came
into our part of the country with the cattle trucks in the

late 1950s. During the transition period when trucks and trains were both used extensively for livestock hauling, hotshots also began to show up at the railroad pens.

The early hotshots were made of metal tubing. They were heavy, some of them nearly three feet long and about an inch and a half in diameter—big enough to accommodate the many large flashlight batteries that powered them. Most of them were dented, evidence of an impatient cowboy who, if the current failed to come through, had used the hotshot as a club.

These early hotshots worked on a shove principle. The handle usually contained a spring; you pushed the hotshot into a cow to complete the circuit. Some models, though, had the spring in the tip, behind a third, extralong prong. Pushing it down evenly with the other two prongs completed the circuit, and you could hear the characteristic loud buzzing.

You didn't need the buzzing, however, to know if a hotshot was working. A hotshotted steer moved quickly enough to tell you that (I should point out that hotshots are humane devices, certainly more humane than clubs or heavy whips).

Today's hotshots carry a battery in the handle and have a long, springy neck made of fiberglass. They are lighter in weight and more flexible than the earlier ones.

I'm not sure just when the hotshot was invented, but not too long ago, I ran across an October, 1902, article in *Popular Mechanics* entitled "Electric Whip." The whip was unquestionably an early hotshot, but its purpose was not for moving cattle. Instead, mailmen were advised to carry one to ward off biting dogs.—*JH*

40. *Working Calves*

IN May, of 1984, I visited Andy Olson, who ranches in the Flint Hills, just south of Council Grove. Andy was getting ready for the modern version of a spring roundup.

He has about six hundred cows, which means, if the bulls have been fertile and the winter not too hard, about six hundred calves to be worked.

Now, "working calves" is a euphemism, probably the most common one. "Making gentlemen out of 'em" is an ironic phrase I've often heard my father use. "Cutting" is the bluntest term, I suppose, while "trimming" is used by the more fastidious. One could also call it "gathering Rocky Mountain oysters."

By whatever term, castrating calves (along with branding, dehorning, and vaccinating) is one of the major annual jobs of any farmer or rancher with more than a few head of mother cows. It is also a job that has a lot of folk custom attached to it, especially the way Andy Olson does it.

Many modern cattlemen will run their calves into a chute and through a calf cradle, a holding device that turns a calf onto his side for the operation. But Andy does it the old-fashioned way—with ropes and horses. His only concessions to modern technology are a set of portable pens and a propane fire for the branding irons.

I arrived about 7:30 on a mid-May morning that was sunny and bright. Meadowlarks were on nearly every fence post, with plover running everywhere through the grass. Cotton Rogers, a transplanted Texan who lives near Cassoday, was just pulling into the pasture, but another half dozen horsemen (and women) were already there, driving about eighty first-calf Angus heifers and their babies into the corner where the pens had been set up.

Richard Miller and Cotton rode into the pen, ropes swinging, and began catching calves. Both were good ropers, but Miller was especially adept at picking up two heels with each throw of the rope, then dragging the calf to the waiting crew.

In fact, there were two crews, neither one of which had much time for waiting. Each calf was earmarked, vaccinated, fly tagged, branded, and, if a bull calf, castrated. The process, if everything went smoothly, took less than a minute. The entire pen of eighty calves was finished in a little less than an hour.

Kenneth Miller, Richard's father, handled the earmarking and tagging. Keith Mahaney, from the Smashed O Ranch, branded. Andy did his own cutting, folding up his knife and putting it into his pocket between calves. Bob Rolhoff, also of the Smashed O, and Wayne Stone, who works full time for Andy, were, along with Chuck Bolles and Rick Fisher, the calf wrestlers. The other two members of the outfit were cowgirls. Bessie Wildman, Andy's sister-in-law, did the vaccinating, while Mandy Olson (Andy's daughter, who is about nine or ten years old) kept the ear-tagging equipment ready.

Working calves in this fashion, with a crew made up primarily of family and neighbors, is an integral part of folk culture not only in Kansas cattle country but throughout the Great Plains. It's a way of sharing work and of having a chance to visit at the same time.—*JH*

41. *Rocky Mountain Oysters*

CERTAIN kinds of food are often associated with certain parts of the country—baked beans with Boston, or crawfish with Louisiana. Beef, of course, is the staple of the Great Plains, but more particularly our special culinary offering is the Rocky Mountain oyster, the polite term for the bovine testicle.

I had never really appreciated that term until the summer of 1983, when our family spent a leisurely week on a boat off the coast of British Columbia. Some mornings, when the tide was out, we would gather oysters. Whether raw, fried, or cooked in the shell over charcoal, these fresh oysters had an exquisite taste, far better than I have ever experienced in a restaurant. It is this richness and delicacy of taste that sea oysters share with the Rocky Mountain variety.

Although the squeamish won't touch them, the aficionado knows that Rocky Mountain oysters are one of the world's great delicacies. Like many things associated with a folk group, names will vary. I have heard them called mountain oysters, prairie oysters, bull fries, and lamb fries. This latter term, I assume, comes from the use of lamb testicles, although it is just as often applied to those from cattle. I have never eaten lamb oysters, but I have tried some from pigs and young goats. I have even heard of turkey fries. Nothing, however, beats genuine calf oysters.

Roundup was the traditional time for gathering mountain oysters in the Great Plains of a century ago. Today most calves are worked before they reach weaning age. While such oysters are smaller, they are also more tender. Another prime gathering time occurs when a rancher has just received a shipment of short yearlings, some or most of which have not yet been castrated.

As the animals are worked, the oysters are tossed into buckets half full of water. Later, the testicles are washed and cleaned of extraneous skin and cords. They are then soaked in salt water overnight. Some people freeze the oysters at this point, reserving final cleaning (i.e., peeling away the outer skin) until the oysters are about one-fourth thawed. This is definitely the easiest way to clean them, but many people prefer fresh oysters to frozen ones. Either way, the next step is to cook them.

Small oysters are best fried whole; large ones must be sliced into pieces that are one-half inch or so thick. Recipes vary, but the best, in my opinion, is the simplest: roll the oyster in a mixture of salt, pepper, and flour and pop it into a skillet of hot grease. Other recipes include batters of Seven-up and pancake flour or of cracker crumbs and butter. Some people deep fry rather than using a frying pan.

Craig Claiborne, of the *New York Times,* credits Helen Dollagan, of the *Denver Post,* with this recipe: soak oysters in milk, dip in fresh bread crumbs, and brown in butter. Serve with ketchup or lemon wedges. To a real plainsman, though, pouring ketchup on good, tender mountain oysters is a sin comparable to smothering a prime, charcoal-broiled, medium-rare T-bone with ketchup.

When I was growing up, we often had mountain oysters for breakfast as a side dish with pancakes. At other times I remember mountain oysters as the main course for informal community gatherings. These were usually stag affairs (no pun intended) at which area ranchers and cowboys would celebrate the end of the calf-working season with a party that would include oysters, beer, and poker.

A few parting words of advice—novice mountain-oyster cooks should be prepared for a strong cooking odor. The cooked oyster will have no trace of this odor, but first-time eaters should be aware that this delicately textured, exquisitely flavored dish is also extremely rich; do not over-eat.—*JH*

Part Four

WORKING

"MAKE HAY WHILE THE SUN SHINES" is the old saying, and the sun definitely shines on the plains in mid-July. Some of the earliest records of agriculture on the Great Plains (not counting the corn and vegetables raised by the Pawnee, Mandan, and other tribes) deal with haying along the Santa Fe Trail. I've recently been rolling up a few bales with my old Allis baler, and it got me to thinking about the haying we used to do when I was growing up.

The jayhawk stacker we used on our Flint Hills stock ranch had a pyramidal frame of four-by-four timbers, and it had a set of about eighteen long, wooden teeth that raised the hay up into the air so that it could be dumped onto the stack. It was drawn by two mules, one on each side of the frame.

My father usually drove the stacker, my uncle stacked, and my grandfather drove the go-devil (some people called it a hay buck or a buck rake). The go-devil was about as wide as the haylift on the stacker and had about the same number of wooden teeth. After depositing a load of hay on the stacker teeth, my grandfather would back off, tip the teeth up by sitting back on the board seat that protruded at the rear, and take off for another load as fast as the mules could trot—"going like the devil!"

When I was small, I spent a lot of time catching horse-flies off the stacker mules and either pulling their heads off or sticking a straw through them and letting them fly away. As I got older, though, I was put on the dump rake. We had acquired a tractor mower fairly early on (although I can still remember seeing my grandfather mow with mules), but we didn't get a side-delivery rake until we bought a round baler in 1952.

My sister and I would take turns raking the alfalfa or prairie-hay fields, then I would usually get the job of raking the "scatterin's" that were left after the go-devil had gone down a windrow.

Still later I graduated to the stacking job (my uncle had moved away and we had had a series of hired helpers in the meantime), but that was after we had bought a farmhand stacker for our tractor. With that bit of automation, we no longer needed the go-devil. The stacker could pick up and dump hay as fast as two people could stack it. No more nice rests while the go-devil was in the far corner of the hayfield!

We continued to stack a lot of hay, especially alfalfa, even after we got our baler. The round prairie-hay bales could be left in the hay meadow until they were needed in the winter, but we didn't have hay barns in which to store our alfalfa. Besides, it was much easier to feed if it had been stacked in a feed rack. That way the cows could come to the alfalfa instead of having to haul it to them.

Today stacking hay is nearly a lost art (I mean building a good round stack that swells out as it goes up from the base, then tapers to a nice point on the top, a stack that is tramped down so that it will turn water ["split a raindrop," my grandfather used to say], and one that can easily be taken apart a forkful at a time). In my travels around the plains in recent years, I have seen very, very few such hay-stacks. The capital-intensive (but labor-saving) big round bale has just about taken over.

I'm glad I had a chance to learn how to stack hay in the traditional way, but I'm not nostalgic or sentimental about it. When I drive past a new-mown field of alfalfa and some-one remarks on the nice smell, I always think of the words I have heard my father say many times: "It smells like work to me."—*JH*

43. *Storing Hay*

GREAT PLAINS farmers and ranchers have employed a variety of hay-preserving methods. As mentioned earlier, we stacked our hay (usually in round stacks, occasionally in loaf form) or used a small round baler.

In some of the plains areas of Wyoming and Montana I've seen the hay derrick, a real attention-getting device used most extensively in Utah and Idaho. The derrick is big enough to be seen from a great distance, is pyramidal in shape, and is made of heavy timbers. It operates as a crane, a long pole serving as a boom to lift the piles of hay so that they can be stacked.

Because of the scarcity of rain in the western Great Plains, hay is sometimes not as carefully stacked there as it is farther east. In the Dakotas and the Nebraska Sandhills I have often seen round metal frames that buckle together. Hay is dumped into these frames, forming a rough stack, then the frame is unbolted, moved to a new location, and fastened again, ready for more hay. Commercial loaf-type haying machines, such as those developed by Hesston, are also used extensively on the High Plains.

In recent years, however, the most successful new hay technology introduced has been the big round baler. This device makes bales of around one thousand pounds. The baler is capital intensive, requiring powerful machinery for every aspect of handling, but the savings in labor expense have made the machine the success it is. No longer does the farmer have to worry about his square bales getting wet because the hay haulers (who charge too much anyway, according to most farmers) can't get to his hay until next Tuesday. Instead he can get a truck load of hay into just a few bales. A fork attachment for his tractor or pickup truck will lift and haul them easily.

For those who still like the traditional square bales (although I could never figure out why a rectangular bale was called square), various types of loaders and stackers have been devised to make hauling easier. Unless they are stacked outside, bales are usually hauled into a pole barn or shed, an open-sided structure with a high tin roof, or into the haymow of a regular barn.

Near Matfield Green, Kansas, is an unusual variation of the traditional hay shed. It is a fairly small (about twenty feet square) structure with a four-sided peaked roof that is adjustable: it raises and lowers. A system of winches, pulleys, and cables allows the roof to be raised to a maximum height of about eighteen feet. The first cutting of alfalfa, for instance, might take up one-third of the space. The roof can then be lowered to keep the rain off the hay until the next cutting is ready, at which point the roof can be raised again. In the winter the roof can be lowered as hay is removed to keep snow from blowing in on the unused hay.

Until about 1983 the only movable-roofed hay barns I had seen were the one in Matfield Green and several in Holland. The Dutch barns tended to be several times larger than the ones in Kansas, a couple of them had thatched roofs, and one was built on three poles instead of four. Otherwise they were the same as the Matfield Green barn.

The movable-roofed hay barn is a clever idea, an appropriate use of folk technology in the preserving of hay. The question is, how did this idea crop up in two locales so far apart and so different in agricultural practice? Was it simply a similar response to a common problem? Or was there some undocumented cause and effect somewhere along the way?—*JH*

44. *The Hay Barrack*

HAY BARNS with movable roofs, I have discovered since 1983, are called "hay barracks," after the Dutch *hooiberg*, which means "hay mountain." In addition to the sheds at Matfield Green, and in Holland, I have also located several dozen in various Kansas counties—Stafford, Reno, Rice, Wilson, and Sedgwick.

The hay barrack at Matfield Green was built by George Deering, who died only a few months ago. He had spent his working life as a welder in the oilfields and, he said, thought up the idea all on his own. The other two hay barracks in Chase County were built by Carl Hansen, who ran a machine shop in Strong City up until the 1950s and ac-

quired the notion of building them in a more traditional
manner—a farmer (Bert Drake, who farms on Diamond
Creek) had seen one in Marion County and took Hansen
over to see it. Hansen told me that he thought that every
farmer and rancher in Chase County would want one, the
idea was so slick. Indeed, everyone who saw his hay barrack
agreed that it was a heck of an idea—but no one, besides
Drake, ordered one.

The area between Maize and Mount Hope, Kansas
(roughly on a line connecting Wichita and Hutchinson),
seems to have the major concentration of Kansas hay barracks. Five of them are on the Woodard farm near Maize,
three are on the Steve Beal farm near Mount Hope, and
there are many, many more in between. Some of these
sheds were seen some thirty years ago by Sam Richardson,
of Stafford, who then went home and built a couple on
his farm.

Allen Noble, of the Pioneer America Society, who has
done extensive study of the hay barrack, tells me that the
origin of this ingenious shed was in the Netherlands, dating
back at least to the fifteenth, perhaps to the thirteenth century. Use of the hay barrack spread to Germany, Austria,
Yugoslavia, and the Ukraine. The barrack appeared in the
American Colonies at least as early as 1733 and has since
been found in Massachusetts, Virginia, Maryland, Ohio,
New York, Rhode Island, Iowa, Illinois, Prince Edward Island, Manitoba, and Newfoundland. As far as I have been
able to determine, the Kansas hay barracks are the first to
be documented west of Iowa.

How did they get here? Folk transmission is difficult to
trace, but two or three theories come to mind. One is spontaneous re-creation, such as happened with George Deering's shed in Matfield Green—matching local needs to local
conditions. More probably, however, the idea accompanied
settlers to the area. German Mennonites, for instance, are
thought to have taken the hay barrack to the Ukraine.
Later some of these same people, along with some Dutch
dairy farmers, immigrated to Kansas, settling in the Arkan-

sas River valley between Hutchinson and Wichita. Whether or not the idea came subconsciously or consciously, it did manifest itself here.

Now, however, many of the hay barracks seem to have outlived their usefulness. Open pole hay barns, dozens of feet high, scores of feet wide, and sometimes over a hundred feet long, are much more efficient storage areas for square bales, while the large round bale has made any indoor storage optional. Raising and lowering the roof of a twenty-by-twenty shed in order to keep a little snow off some hay that will soon be fed anyway is, apparently, no longer economically desirable.

Still, I hope not all the hay barracks here will be scrapped or allowed to disintegrate. They are living examples of agricultural folklife.—*JH*

45. *Cool Water*

ANYONE who has spent any time at all outdoors in the plains during summertime has gotten thirsty. I don't know how many people are like me, but I can remember several times when I would have given almost anything for a drink of water. And I've had a couple of drinks that were downright memorable.

I remember especially the water jugs we took to the fields when we were haying or threshing or cultivating. The jugs were usually gallon or half-gallon size and made of glass or crockery, each one wrapped in denim or burlap to soak up excess water and thus provide some cooling by evaporation. Sometimes we would fill them from the faucet at the house, but if the wind was blowing, we would fill them with cold water from the windmill.

The ice-filled insulated plastic and metal coolers we have today certainly keep water much colder than did those cloth-wrapped jugs, but I don't think anyone who has drunk from both kinds will dispute my belief that a few swallows of cool or lukewarm water from a jug are much more satisfying than any amount of ice-cold water from a cooler. Ice water might taste better at the moment of drinking, but it just doesn't satisfy thirst the way jug water does.

Haying and threshing were always hot, dusty jobs, so we always had plenty of water on hand. Other times, however, you could get caught without a jug and get pretty thirsty. We had one place a couple of miles from home where we usually raised milo or kaffir for shock feed, a quarter section with, I suppose, about sixty acres broken out and the rest in pasture. Some of the rows were half a mile long, and cultivating new sorghum was a slow process. On a cool, early-June morning, I would not often think of taking a water jug with me (kids usually had better things to think of anyway), but by eleven o'clock or so, especially if the sun was bearing down, I would be spitting cotton.

There was a windmill in the pasture next to the field, and if I was within a quarter mile of it, I would sometimes just have to shut off the tractor and go for a drink. Talk about good water—cold and fresh after being drawn up through sixty feet of Flint Hills limestone! Unless, as happened too many times, the wind had stopped blowing just about the time I got there. Of course, it would always start blowing again—just about the time I got back to the tractor.

Spitting cotton. The first time I heard that expression, I was about eight or nine years old and we were shipping cattle. The grownups didn't seem to mind, but my sister and I would really get thirsty on that long drive from the pastures east of town to the Cassoday stockyards. Our last chance for a drink was at a spring that flowed in Harsh's Hill Pasture, about ten or twelve miles from town. From then on it was a dry drive, and in late July that meant hot, dusty, and thirsty.

I remember one time we took cattle out on the Teterville Road and headed straight west into the yards instead of cutting across pastures. There was a windmill close to the road, pumping out of an old hand-dug well, and I crawled through the fence and went over for a drink. It was a drink I remember well, for I looked down into the well after I had finished and saw a snake swimming around. I don't think I have drunk from a hand-dug well since then. I know that I didn't get thirsty any more on that particular drive.—*JH*

46. *Binder Harvest*

I RECEIVED a telephone message from Jerry Paige that the boys in Goessel were ready to start binding wheat. This communication seemed a half-century or more out of its historical place. It reminded me of the annual calls that used to issue successively from each of the plains states to summon a corps of harvest hands during the days prior to the advent of the combine.

Still, in far-separated parts of the plains bits of grain are bound and set aside, because scores of communities from Perryton, Texas, to Saskatoon, Saskatchewan, sponsor old-time threshing bees. That's the case with Goessel, where the Mennonite Museum convenes its Threshing Days each August.

Early in the June evening I started for Goessel, driving the county roads to make better time, flocks of turtle doves boiling up in front of me, dust behind. The evening cool set herds of longhorns grazing on hillsides—not ghost herds from a historian's fantasy, but flesh-and-blood longhorns, the breed again a common sight in cattle-breeding country, because longhorn bulls make slender calves and easy first calving.

Sleek Gleaners plied the grain fields. Their activity, and the mulberries hanging ripe along the roadside, indicated to me that it might be a little late to start a binder harvest.

As I hit the edge of Goessel, LeAnn Toews waved at me, and I got guidance from her as to where the binding was going on. We found the patch, about an acre, already half cut. There was only one binder, hitched to a little Ford tractor, and there were eight or ten shockers, so fellows were standing around waiting for bundles to drop from the carrier.

I watched the geometry of binding and shocking unfold speedily. The binder, in the course of its rounds, laid down piles of bundles in rows perpendicular to its line of travel. The shockers consolidated the piles into shocks along the same rows. They seemed to know what they were doing. They began each shock by grasping by the twine a bundle in each hand, then thumping the two bundles smartly together in upright position, heads up. Three piles of bundles, perhaps twelve bundles altogether, made a shock.

The wheat was a little greener than what the neighbors were combining; it was about right for binding. The heads on the standing stalks were unbowed; the bundles handled nicely. The binding and shocking finished up as the low sun stretched the interlocking shadows of the shocks into a chain across the field.

If this were a true precombine harvest scene, then the exhausted shockers would be slumping back to the farmhouse for supper and rest. Instead, they were lingering and drinking Cokes. If these truly were old-time harvest hands, they would be a mixture of Arkies and other poor farmers from the Mississippi valley and college boys out of school for the summer. The group was diverse enough, but the elements in the mix were wrong—several local farmers, a few men with jobs in town, and counting me, three college professors.

What were they doing there? They were re-creating tradition. I say "re-creating" and not "perpetuating." In the presence of modern agricultural science, people cannot pass on in unbroken perpetuity a set of customs based on obsolete technology. They can, however, re-create them. What I observed at Goessel was not exactly harvesting. It was more like a living photograph, a treasured image placed on display but once a year.—*TI*

47.   *Shocking Wheat*

SINCE the coming of the combine, a generation of farmers who have never shocked wheat has grown up on the plains. Lest this traditional activity become a lost craft, I began asking old-timers to record for me how they made shocks.

I found first of all that I had to get my terms straight. People on the southern plains talk about "shocking" wheat, but residents of the northern plains speak of "stooking." I'm not sure where the geographic division between the two usages is, but I suspect it is about at the line dividing the spring wheat region from the winter wheat region. I am also curious about the possible ethnic origins of the word "stook."

There was some regional variation as to how many bundles properly went into a shock. In most places eight was considered a good number, but this may have been more a function of how many bundles the carrier on the binder held than of personal preference. Professor J. A. Boan, a farm boy turned economist now at the University of Regina, Saskatchewan, tells me eight was the standard number in his stooking days. Several people from Kansas concur. But Milo Mathews, who grew up making eight-bundle stooks in Iowa, says that when he worked in the Dakotas, the people there put more bundles in a shock to hold it against the wind.

A similar logic prevailed on the question of capsheaves. In the Midwest, once the shocker had stood up the proper number of bundles, he took one more, held it between his legs, spread the two ends of it, and placed it atop the shock to turn the rain. On the plains, most shockers agreed that capsheaves just blew away in the wind anyway.

Different individuals handled bundles in different ways. Michael Ewanchuk, a historian from Manitoba, says he picked up two sheaves at a time, one under each arm. Obviously he would have to shift them to his extended hands to set them up. Most shockers just grabbed the bundles by the twine, one in each hand. A few used a three-tined fork, but that seems cumbersome to me. Ewanchuk says he used a fork for barley, and considering how scratchy barley is, that makes sense.

Not uncommonly the binder failed to tie a bundle. In such a case it was the shocker's duty to twist a handful of stalks into a cord with which to tie up the sheaf, the same way all bundles were tied in the days of cradles and scythes or reapers, before the advent of the binder.

A shock of eight bundles was begun by leaning two together, the heads meeting at the top, the butts apart at the bottom. Next the shocker leaned two more bundles against the first two, all the heads together, the angle of the first pair perpendicular to the angle of the second pair as viewed from above. The following four bundles fit into the corners between the first four.

A twelve-bundle shock was begun the same way, but the second pair of bundles was leaned alongside of and parallel to the first pair. Then the third pair was leaned in from the perpendicular direction. It was like seating six people at an oblong table, two on each side and one on each end. The remaining six bundles were leaned into the corners between the first six.

It must have been satisfying to look out across a field full of shocks standing as neat as biscuits on a baking sheet.—*TI*

48. *Harvest Hands*

THE annual wheat harvest on the plains is an exhilarating time. Get the chaff out of your eyes, and it's exciting to see those combines shaking through the fields and those grain trucks flying through stoplights to get a place in line at the elevator.

But it's a nervous time, too, because the harvest is a race against the elements to save the year's crop. Wheat won't wait. The pressure can cause all sorts of conflicts and breakdowns.

Nowhere was this more true than in the relations between farmers and harvest hands in the days prior to the advent of the combine. Some people have fond memories of particular harvest hands, but by and large, farmers were only too happy to replace the bindlestiffs, as some called them, with combines.

One reason was that farmers considered the bindlestiffs unreliable. The crop was just not as important to the hands as it was to the farmer. If they became displeased or even just bored, they might walk off the job, perhaps even before they began work.

William Lies, who grew up on a farm near Cathay, North Dakota, told me, "As a kid I used to think it was great when a man who was hired stayed overnight for supper and breakfast and then went back to town. My mother would call the police and tell him to collect for the two meals." I suppose that was kind of exciting, but it didn't get the wheat cut.

Farmers became especially suspicious—often unjustifiably so—when rumors of IWW organizers went around. "IWW" stood officially for "Industrial Workers of the World," but lots of farmers said that what it really meant was "I Won't Work" or "I Want Wine."

Lies said one of his neighbors had some trouble with a group of hands he suspected of IWW sympathies, pulled out a revolver, and said, "I'll give you SOB's five minutes to get off the place!" For the next few nights after they left, though, someone slept under the separator to guard it against sabotage.

Farm women especially disliked having harvest hands on the place because they were a bad moral influence. A prominent educator who grew up in north-central Kansas gave me six verses to a song called "Lulu" taught him by a harvest hand. ("Lulu" was an old cowboy song that made the rounds among other occupational groups.) Those rhymes are the filthiest I have ever seen—great folklore, but filthy. Sorry I can't print them.

The difference in point of view that I've been talking about is pretty well summarized in a poem sent to me by Guy Bretz, who lives in Buffalo, Missouri, but grew up in Lane County, Kansas. His father was a thresherman as well as a farmer. The poem, recited to him by a harvest hand in 1915, goes like this:

> The farmer stood on the wheat stack,
> The hobo sat on the ground.
> Says the hobo to the farmer,
> "Will you quit when the sun goes down?"
> "Hell, no," says the farmer,
> "We'll work as long as it's light."
> Says the hobo to the farmer,
> "Give me my time tonight.
> I'll roam this wide world over,
> I'll travel from town to town,
> Until I find some damned old farmer
> That will quit when the sun goes down."—*TI*

49. *Eating Like a Harvest Hand*

I REMEMBER when I was growing up that if my sister and I were really shoveling our food down, we were never told that we were eating like a pig or a horse; rather, we were told: "Slow down. You're eating like a harvest hand." Our stock ranch was not in wheat country, but we did raise oats regularly when I was growing up, and I remember a couple of times when we had some wheat.

I also remember threshing. In fact, I remember it too well. I was plenty old enough to shock oats and help haul bundles to the separator before we finally got a combine.

Threshing was fun when I was little. That meant that there would be lots of neighbors there, with lots of horses and mules that were different from ours, and, once I had helped dress several chickens, I could take the dogs and go out to the field where the men were loading wagons. The mice were thick under those shocks, and the dogs and I did our best to make the world safe for people who were afraid of mice.

When I was older, though, the fun left. Shocking oats was hot, itchy work, and so was threshing. I learned then the reason for the term "eating like a harvest hand." We had earned the right to eat quickly and ravenously.

At home I remember mainly having fried chicken or roast beef as the main course, with potatoes and gravy, corn, green beans, tomatoes, cabbage—whatever was abundant in the garden at that time. We always had iced tea with the meal, and we would take our water jugs to the windmill just before we went back to the field and fill them with fresh, cold well water.

But to get back to the eating. When my mother was a girl, she used to help cook for the harvest crew that my grandfather (Ben Rice, of Conway Springs, Kansas) hired for his custom threshing outfit. Sometimes, she said, Grandpa would go into town in the morning to hire workers. Most of them were good hands (one came from Missouri every year to help for the season), but a few would come out, eat breakfast, work none too hard until noon, eat a big meal (like a real harvest hand), and then walk back into town. They never got hired again, at least not by Grandpa, but then they didn't really care.

Recently I talked with Velma O'Bryan, of El Dorado, Kansas. Her father, Wes King, lived near Burns when she was a girl, and she remembers that when she was about ten or eleven years old he had a big wheat crop and bought a steam engine and a separator. For the next several years he did custom threshing for the neighborhood, and Flora King and her daughter did the cooking. "We had fried chicken sometimes," she told me, "but usually Mother would cut slices of salt pork she had packed, soak it awhile to take out some of the salt, then roll it in flour and fry it.

When you got outside of a few slices of that, you knew you had some meat."

Along with the fried pork, the Kings would serve potatoes and gravy, navy or lima beans, another vegetable (often cooked cabbage), fresh-baked bread, home-churned butter, lots of coffee, and pie. When the men were threshing kaffir corn, pumpkins would sometimes be in season, and they would have pumpkin pie. Usually, however, it was fruit pie.

The hot slaw that Flora King made was a real favorite of all the threshers that helped her father, Mrs. O'Bryan told me. The cabbage was shredded just as it would be for regular slaw, then it was boiled with salt, pepper, and butter—cooked just enough to make it a little soft.

Mrs. O'Bryan also told me about making some apricot pies once for threshers. She was helping a neighbor lady cook, and she was told she had to get a number of pies— four or five—out of one can of apricots. When she opened the can, however, it was fully one-half juice; very few apricots. But she had to make it do, so "I added lots of thickening," she told me, "and they ate every bite and never complained a bit." Of course not—they were hungry as harvest hands, weren't they?—*JH*

50. *The Combine Comes to the Plains*

WE people of the plains think of ourselves as self-reliant and of our home region as distinctive, and rightly so. Yet few of the things that come to mind as symbols of the Great Plains—windmills, barbed wire, and so on—originated within the region. Rather they were inventions from other places that plainsmen adapted to their own purposes and then embraced as their own.

Such was the case with the combined harvester, or combine. Although in contemporary times combines have reached their highest state on the plains, the first one was the invention of Hiram Moore and John Hascall of Kalamazoo County, Michigan, in the late 1830s.

The combine never caught on in Michigan, probably because of competition from the simpler, cheaper reapers of Obed Hussey and Cyrus McCormick, but also because the combine was more suited to places where the weather at harvest was more dependably dry.

So in 1854 two partners, George Leland and Andrew Moore (no relation to the inventor), shipped a combine around Cape Horn to California. With it they did custom work on the wheat ranches of the central valley. They had trouble from the start collecting on bad debts, and then a fire resulting from failure to lubricate the machine destroyed it.

Wheat ranchers (funny how people in Texas and California call their operations "ranches" even when they don't have a head of stock on the place) in California liked the new machine, though, and despite protests from harvest workers, local mechanics built more combines. From these origins sprang the enterprises of Daniel Best and Benjamin Holt, pioneer manufacturers of combines that won the western wheatlands of California and Washington.

These were mammoth machines pulled by as many as thirty-two horses or mules, the driver perched on a ladderseat above the animals, the threshing parts driven from a ground wheel.

Such ungainly gleaners were never popular east of the Rockies. Well into the twentieth century farmers on the plains remained happy with their binders, headers, and stationary threshers—until World War I, when the demands of war produced both a wheat boom and a labor shortage. The expansion of wheat farming continued into the 1920s, worsening the harvest bottleneck and creating more need for combines.

Still, two more things had to happen before combines came to the plains. First, because farmers here rejected combines that threshed with power from ground wheels, manufacturers put on auxiliary engines to do the threshing. Engine-equipped combines of moderate size, ten to sixteen feet, were called "prairie models." These worked much better under the grain and ground conditions of the plains, but nevertheless, farmers remained skeptical of hitching engine-driven machines behind horses for motive power.

Fortunately, tractors, the second element necessary for adoption of combines, arrived on the plains in the early 1920s. With the advent of tractors, combines also won acceptance. "Once over and it's all over" was the motto of wheat men on the southern high plains, who welcomed the machine that finally opened the harvest bottleneck.

Farther north, in the spring wheat region, the combine had to be adapted still more before it suited farmers' needs—but that's another story.—*TI*

51. *The Harvest Brigade*

WORLD WAR I, I wrote earlier, was a big reason why farmers adopted the combine for harvesting. It's obvious that the location of the Great Plains squarely in the middle of North America has provided no insulation from the heat of America's foreign wars, but just as obvious that not all the effects of war on the plains have been bad.

Both world wars stimulated better prices for grain, and both brought technical advances to agriculture. The institution of custom combining, for instance, which has served grain farmers well for a generation and a half, was largely a product of World War II.

During the war farmers produced the greatest wheat crops in the nation's history to that time, but government allocation of steel left them short on implements to harvest the bumper crops. Custom combining, which made maximum use of each machine by moving it north with the progression of the harvest, was a logical solution. Custom combining eased shortages of both machinery and labor. It survived the war to become a perennial part of harvest on the plains.

The most colorful incident in the early history of custom combining was the Harvest Brigade, or more formally, the Massey-Harris Self-Propelled Harvest Brigade. This occurred in 1944, when the governments of the United States and Canada, although they wouldn't admit it then, already were shifting resources away from military production and toward civilian needs of the coming postwar era.

At this time Massey-Harris Company approached both governments with a proposal to help save the abundant harvest of 1944 by putting five hundred No. 21 self-propelled combines into the hands of custom combiners. The Canadian government gave the company the steel, Massey-Harris produced the machines, and the company shipped them south to such cities as Enid and Hutchinson for sale to custom harvesters, each of whom had to pledge to combine at least five hundred acres that year.

Since everything done during the war was a "victory" project, the Harvest Brigade assumed a military organization, at least on paper. The head of Massey-Harris's American operations was General of the Harvest Brigade, company mechanics were Technical Sergeants, custom harvesters were Lieutenants, and so on. The company offered war bonds as prizes for harvesters who covered the most acres.

There was an emormous amount of hoopla associated with the Harvest Brigade, because Massey-Harris knew that the project was a promoter's dream. Jubilant press releases and stirring photographs filled the nation's papers. The company even made a pretty good documentary movie, *Wonder Harvest,* about the effort. (Well, maybe the movie was a little propagandistic, but it still was better than the popular motion picture romance, *Wild Harvest,* produced a couple of years later by Paramount. *Wild Harvest* starred Alan Ladd and Robert Preston opposite Dorothy Lamour as, so the notices said, a "Sizzling Siren of the Prairies.")

In the aggregate, the Harvest Brigade fulfilled its promise, combining more than a million acres. Massey-Harris probably profited most from the venture. Its No. 21 SP was the most popular combine in the wheat belt for several years thereafter.

. The custom cutters, meanwhile, made enough money to get a good start in the business before the price of wheat broke in 1948. Their sons and daughters and grandchildren carry on the enterprise today.—*TI*

52. *Milking Cows*

NOT too many years ago you could find a few milk cows on nearly every farm and ranch in the Great Plains. Even in the small towns there was usually someone who kept a few cows in a nearby pasture and peddled the fresh milk to his neighbors. Only in fairly recent times have specialized dairy farms and supermarkets conspired to force pasteurized, homogenized milk on us all. Just think of the loss—generations of farm kids (and millions of farm cats) who will never know the taste of fresh, warm milk squirted directly from cow to mouth.

But I believe that even staunch libertarians would prefer a few USDA cleanliness regulations to the way I used to do the milking. I found the chore extremely boring and tiresome, so I would liven things up by trying to squirt flies or chunks of barnyard dirt into the foam on the top of the milk.

Like many people on the rural plains, we kept some whole milk for our own use, then separated the cream from the rest and sold it to a creamery truck that stopped a couple of times a week. The driver would pick up our cream and leave cheese and butter. My earliest memories are of a hand-cranked cream separator. Along with the wringer washing machine, the electric separator was one of the great laborsaving devices to come to rural America.

We fed our skim milk to bucket calves (some people fed

pigs with theirs). I remember how glad I was when we quit selling cream and bought some extra calves to put on the milk cows. No more milking, no more lugging full buckets all the way from the barn to the house for separating, then lugging full buckets all the way back to the barn and beyond to the calf pen. We would often have three or four calves on a cow, then wean them and raise another two or three with the same cow before she went dry. I don't know which way made more money, but I sure preferred letting the calves do all the work.

Milking wasn't all bad, though. I really liked getting on the horse and riding out for the cows in the evening. And I liked sitting down to an easy milker, sinking my head in her flank, and losing myself in thought. If you haven't mused while milking, you have never enjoyed real contemplation. Also, as my friends and I grew older and thought we wanted to compete in rodeos, the old milk cows were an easier (and cheaper) lesson than entering a real bull riding.

But milking had some drawbacks, too. I hated to put kickers on, and we always had a couple of cows that needed them. Then there was the swishing of tails. A plain old tail whipped around the back of your head and across your face was bad enough, but even worse was one filled with cockleburs. Worst of all was the tail of a cow that had been running in rich new spring grass. And I really hated to get the cows of a morning. Mornings came so early on the farm, and the dew seemed always heavy and cold.

Still I'm thinking of buying a cow next spring. Milking is an experience my kids really ought to have.—*JH*

Part Five

PLAYING

IN LATE JULY, of 1984, our family went to see the Kansas City Royals play the Baltimore Orioles. The kids got to see George Brett play, and Willie Wilson, Dan Quisenberry, Eddie Murray, Cal Ripken, Jr.—surely some hall-of-famers in that bunch somewhere.

The only other time I saw a professional baseball game was in 1953, Stan Musial and the St. Louis Cardinals beating Cincinnati. Now thirty-one years might seem like a long time between games, considering that I enjoyed myself both times, but it's a little hard for me to get overly excited about something that puts about ten minutes of action into a package of over three hours. In fact, if hanging is supposed to concentrate the mind, a baseball game would certainly unconcentrate it.

There were nearly twenty-nine thousand people in Royals Stadium, of whom maybe one thousand were trying to pay close attention to the action. The rest, it seemed, were just having a good time—drinking pop and beer, eating hotdogs and snow cones, talking to friends, cheering the home team. So after a while I, too, quit trying to follow the action, relaxed, and had fun like everyone else.

Actually it was a bit difficult to follow the action anyway from our bleacher seats in right field. At that distance everything—the players, the hits, the fielding—had a kind of remoteness, a purified, romantic quality. Maybe it was because we couldn't see all the tobacco spitting that television brings up close in living color.

I'm afraid that my lack of enthusiasm for baseball would have made me an oddity during the first few decades of this century. Nearly every town on the plains had its baseball team, and every half-dozen or so towns would form a league.

My hometown organized a team at least as early as 1907. The photographs I have seen indicate that it was a classy and serious endeavor—spiffy uniforms, good equipment, stern demeanors on the faces of the players. Cassoday played teams from the surrounding area—Burns, Wonsevu, Matfield Green. From what I have heard, however, not many of the Matfield Green games went the full nine innings—too many fistfights.

Another diversion in early ball games on the Great Plains was the impromptu rodeo. I have seen an old photograph (from Sand Springs, Oklahoma) showing a bronc being ridden on the infield during the seventh-inning stretch. I know that Turk Harsh, from Cassoday, and Andy Torrance and Vic Kirk, from Matfield Green, often would bring broncs to the ball games, sometimes riding between almost every two innings. Or between fights!

I don't know of any roping or bulldogging at these early baseball games, but I would not be surprised to learn of some. Baseball might have been almost a mania in early twentieth-century rural America, but horse sports were the indigenous games of the Great Plains.

In fact, when I was researching the rodeo held as part of the entertainment at the Field Day at Burdick, Kansas (a fall festival much like today's county fairs; it ran from 1910 to 1923), I found that many of the same names that appeared on the list of winners in the bronc riding and steer roping also stood out prominently in the stats of the baseball games held earlier in the day.

Today, it seems, slow-pitch softball has replaced baseball as the popular game in plains towns, and pizza and beer after the game have taken the place of the seventh-inning bronc rides.—*JH*

54. *Broncs and Baseball*

EARLIER I wrote about baseball on the plains in the early part of this century and about some of the players who were also cowboys. One of the most interesting of these was Harry Person, of Burdick, Kansas.

Person is in his eighties and is still alive, well, and living in Paris, Arkansas. In his youth Harry was a bronc rider and a baseball pitcher, and his brother Dave was a roper. Dave would work during the summer in the open-range country near Tucumcari, New Mexico, then come back to his hometown to win the steer roping there and at other rodeos in the area.

In the spring of 1916 Harry Person took off for Big Sky country, breaking horses for the army at Fort Keough, Montana. These horses were range horses from Wyoming, but not mustangs. They were ranch-bred, castrated as colts, then turned loose to run free for three or four years.

They were big and they were wild. Harry remembers seeing them come into Fort Keough in railroad stockcars in late spring, so nervous that they had chewed holes through the boards of the cars. Their winter hair had all shed off, except for a long strip down the center of their foreheads. Harry says that it was an intimidating sight for a young kid who thought he was a rider—those wild horses with their heads sticking out of the holes they had gnawed in the boards, long hanks of hair flapping from their foreheads.

Army personnel unloaded the horses and got a halter on each one. At the bottom of the unloading chute they handed the halter rope to the civilian horsebreaker. From that moment on the horse was his until it was tamed. Usually he could get his bronc pulled into the barn and tied up by himself, but sometimes the breakers had to help each other with that job.

The commander wanted the horses gentled, not broken, but, Harry remembers, there was little anyone could do to stop the horses from bucking—except to ride it out of them. The parade ground was where the breaking occurred, and it was chopped up something terrible from all the pounding hooves.

Each horsebreaker had eight horses at any one time, and he rode each one an hour each day. Harry remembers that he usually managed to break about twelve horses a month. For that work he was paid $45—in gold. These horses, once gèntled, were shipped by train to El Paso, where the cavalry was engaged in a little skirmish with a Mexican dissident named Pancho Villa.

One night, however, the post commander saw Harry throwing a baseball, and he soon was making his $45 a month but riding only half the horses. The rest of the day he was playing baseball, the only civilian member of the post team.

Harry returned to Burdick in October, 1916, finishing second in the bronc riding that year to rodeo clown and professional bronc rider Si Perkins. The next year he was in France, part of the American Expeditionary Force.

After the war Harry stayed in Europe with the occupational troops. While there he continued to play army baseball, and one of the men he competed against was a Nebraska farm boy who later ended up in the Baseball Hall of Fame—Grover Cleveland Alexander. Quite a set of experiences for a young Kansas cowboy.—*JH*

55. *Six-Man Football*

BACK in the 1930s most small high schools played only one extramural sport, basketball. Football, although immensely popular, required so many players that the small schools either could not assemble a team or had to field such young boys that they were liable to be injured. And football was expensive, entailing costs for equipment and for transportation of the team.

Then came six-man, the football game of the plains. Stephen E. Epler, of the Beatrice, Nebraska, High School, is credited as the originator of the game. His idea was to cut the size of the team by eliminating the guards and tackles—the "drudgery and colorless positions," he called them—and one back, making a six-man team on which everyone but the center was eligible to receive a forward pass.

Two other key rules distinguished six-man football

from the eleven-man variety. First, the field size was reduced to forty yards by eighty yards. Second, before the offense could cross the line of scrimmage with the ball, it had to execute a three-yard "clear pass," essentially a lateral. On September 16, 1934, some boys from Chester and Hardy, Nebraska, met some boys from Belvidere and Alexandria, Nebraska, on the Hebron College Field in the first organized six-man football contest. That same fall a few school principals in Barnes County, North Dakota, agreed to begin six-man practice and to play a few exhibition contests.

The following year principals from schools on both sides of the Kansas-Nebraska border formed the Little Blue Six Man Football League and played a full schedule. The North Dakotans did likewise, staging many of their contests in Valley City, a central location for the schools involved.

The six-man format proved practical and appealing in those days before widespread school consolidation. Leagues quickly organized from North Dakota to Texas. From the plains the game spread to small schools in the Midwest and South.

Although its originators intended that six-man ball should be as similar to eleven-man as possible, the six-man game had its own character. Neither the early players nor their coaches knew how to tackle low, and so scores ran high—eighty points were not an uncommon production for two teams. It was a game of mobility more than brawn. Shifty little 120-pound halfbacks skirted the ends and left heavy linemen behind.

Most of all, the game was flashy. With the required lateral, and with the forward pass quickly proven the best manner of moving the ball up the sparsely-populated field, every play seemed razzle-dazzle to spectators accustomed to three-yards-and-a-cloud-of-dust in the eleven-man game.

Six-man was fun, and it had its place in sports history, but it had no future. As school consolidation accelerated during the 1950s, the consolidated schools generally switched to eleven-man or at least to eight-man (which still looks to me like a pretty wide-open game). People watching the game for the first time tell me that it looks more like fast-break basketball than standard football.

Six-man football, product of the plains, persisted on the plains longer than in other regions, largely because the factor of distance delayed consolidation here. A few schools in Nebraska and in Montana still play it, but the only state where many do is Texas, where more than sixty schools continue to play six-man.—*TI*

56. *Swings*

SWINGS are universal playthings for children, even on the treeless plains. Old tires are often recycled into swings by hanging them from a rafter (or a tree limb, if one is available). Another common recycling results in the gunnysack swing. Take a gunnysack, fill it with hay (or, if you're from West Texas, with cotton), tie it with a rope, and swing it from a tree. The major construction problem today is in finding a gunnysack—cow feed now usually comes in paper sacks, grass seed in plastic ones.

When I was growing up, we stored loose hay, not bales, in the barn, so our favorite place for one of these swings was in the haymow. Sailing off a gunnysack swing onto a big pile of soft hay was a little dusty but a genuine thrill. Another name for the gunnysack swing is the "pappy-dad." Where it got this name, or why, I have no idea. I would certainly welcome any theories.

Speaking of names brings me to the second type of swing—the goat swing of Norton, Kansas. I first heard of the goat swing from my sister-in-law, Carolyn Kruse, who had visited friends at Norton. As part of her entertainment while there, she was taken out to swing on the goat swing.

According to one woman from Norton, the swing itself was a long cable fastened to the top of a huge elm tree on the bank of a creek where local residents often went for picnics. The seat of the swing was a disc of wood with the cable run through and knotted. To ride, you grabbed the rope (or cable) and tried to get on the seat as you went swinging out over the creek. The rope was long and the water a fair distance down; the danger of falling in made the ride scary (and exciting).

No one knows who put up the original goat swing at Norton, but it was done around the turn of the century on the old Rhodes place. Besides enduring thousands of thrill seekers, the old swing also survived a tornado in 1965 that flipped it up into the top of the tree. The tree, however, succumbed to Dutch elm disease a few years back.

Today, though, there are four goat swings on the Donovan farm, which has had some on the place for half a century. Nearly all the young people from the area have, at one time or another, swung on the swings while picnicking.

As for the name, one informant told me that you have to be as agile and surefooted as a goat to reach the swing, which is located in a pasture. Another told me that if you accidentally fall from the swing into the creek, you are the goat, the butt of the joke.

The goat swing is a normal part of life at Norton, and residents consider the term a generic one for any similar swing. One resident noted that the television commercials for Mountain Dew a few years back featured a goat swing— a group of children swimming in a rural swimming hole, some of them swinging out over the water and dropping in.

Certainly this type of swing can be found in almost any area where young people can find trees and water. But only in Norton have I heard it called a "goat swing."—*JH*

57. *Winter Fun*

DECEMBER, 1983, was one of the coldest and snowiest we have had here in the Flint Hills for several years. Even before winter officially began, we had experienced several consecutive days of sub-zero weather and a snow accumulation of nine or ten inches—with more of both to follow as it turned out.

I don't know if winters tend to be milder now than they used to be or if I just remember more snow when I was growing up. But it looks like 1983 will be a winter that will allow our children to say when they grow up, "It sure doesn't snow like it used to." A good, old-fashioned winter isn't all bad, though. It reminds me of the fun we used to have in the ice and snow, before anyone had ever heard of snowmobiles or cross-country skiing.

Ice skating held a great attraction for plains inhabitants in the earlier years of this century, judging from the number of key-adjustable skates one sees at auctions and in antique stores. I remember as a kid trying to fit an old pair onto my work shoes so I could try the ice. I did try a few times, but never successfully. Dad, though, talks about skating parties at night with a bonfire on the bank of the creek. Or about playing hockey with hedge or hickory sticks and a tin can for a puck (thereby transferring shinny to ice in a reversal of the probable origin of that game of speed, endurance, and pain).

Our favorite snow-time recess game in grade school was fox and geese (our favorite, that is, except for building snow forts and pelting each other with snowballs). It's been so long that I don't remember all the rules, but I do remember the big circle in the snow with spokes radiating from the center, where the geese would be safe. It seems like either the fox or the geese could travel in only one direction. I remember, too, that if we had a large number playing, we would have two concentric circles in addition to the center area and the spokes. That gave us a lot of room for maneuvering.

Snow time was also great for trapping rabbits in box traps. Grandpa Rice made one for me when I was in grade school, a long rectangular box with a sliding door at one end held up by an arrangement of sticks and string that would, when a rabbit entered the box after the bait, trip and let the door down. We ate a few of the rabbits I caught, but most of them got turned loose to be trapped again.

When I got older and started rodeoing, I envied the guys who lived on the southern plains and could rope all winter. That's one thing you don't do in the snow—unless you have an indoor arena. But I did learn one summer from a friend who had been working on a Montana ranch about winter bronc riding. They would buck horses out of a chute into a snow-filled arena. When the broncs got bogged down in a drift, the rider would step off and un-saddle. A good illustration of why top bronc riders tend to come from the north country, ropers from the southwest.

Nowadays, although I don't mind dallying a rope around the saddle horn and giving the kids a good brisk sled ride, my favorite winter sport is watching a good fire in the fire-place.—*JH*

58. *Butcher's Art*

FOLKLORISTS like me love to analyze the cultural trappings carried to the North American Great Plains by the many European immigrants who settled here. Ethnic food customs are good examples of these transplanted European-isms. One of the most peculiar of these food customs, especially to modern consumers accustomed to viewing their meat through cellophane, was the craft of decorative meat cutting.

One butcher who practiced this folk art was Karl Tews, with whom I talked in Hastings, Nebraska. He was born in 1906 in Cammin, Germany (now a part of Poland), where his family operated a slaughterhouse. After his father was killed in World War I, and after postwar inflation set in, the family sold the business. So Tews apprenticed with another butcher until 1923, when he emigrated to the United States.

Landing in New York, he traveled to Omaha and thence to Hastings, where he began working for Karl Kauf. Kauf, also a German immigrant, owned a butcher shop called the

Union Market. Tews was to become Kauf's right-hand man and work for him for twenty years.

For Tews and the rest of Kauf's men, each week's work was much the same as the previous week's. On Monday they made sausage, feeding the grinder with ingredients according to their traditional recipes, filling cases with the stuffer. On Tuesday they killed hogs. On Wednesday they made sausage again, and on Thursday they killed hogs again. On Friday morning they butchered cattle. On Friday afternoon they dressed chickens, hundreds of them, so that their customers could have chicken after church on Sunday. On Saturday they rendered lard and cured meat.

With a routine like that, it was little wonder that the men seized any opportunity they had to be festive. Tews had some experience decorating hams for weddings in Germany, but in Hastings he found that when Christmas neared, his fellow German butchers made gaily decorated beef carcasses a holiday specialty.

The craft was not difficult for a skilled cutter, Tews explained. First, he said, "You just have a couple of drinks and close one eye." Then he cut the flank of the hanging beeve so that it would drop, loosening the muscles over which he was preparing to carve. This done, with a sharp knife he began paring away from the surface of the carcass bits of fat shaped like flowers, leaves, or whatever pattern struck his fancy. Cutting away the fat exposed the red lean below to form a red-and-white design.

The decorated beeves hanging in the market might be festooned with garlands and holly, the better to raise the holiday spirits of customers tripping through the sawdust to examine the carcasses.—*TI*

59. *Christmas on the Prairie*

I HAVE noticed that at this time of year people of a certain age often start conversations with words like "Christmas has really changed. Why, I remember when there was noth-

ing in my stocking but an orange. . . ." And then the competition to see who had the most deprived (yet the hap-
piest) Christmas begins. I hate to think that I have reached
that certain age, but I do find myself thinking more now
about Christmases past than I did a few years ago.

I got to thinking about them during the Christmas of
1983 when my son, Josh, and I saddled up our horses,
grabbed a bow saw and a rope, and rode into the timber to
search for a nice cedar. Our fall had been warm and wet
here in the Flint Hills, so the cedars were green and fresh,
not red and dry. We found a good one and dragged it
home, just like in all those paintings of cowboy Christmases
from Texas to Canada.

One thing I remember especially well from my childhood is drawing names at school for exchanging Christmas
presents. I don't recall a single gift I got, but I do remember drawing those names.

In many rural areas the main Christmas program is put
on by the schools, but at Cassoday the event everyone
looked forward to was the Christmas Eve program at the
one church in town (Methodist). Most of the town turned
out for it, especially the families with children. Everyone
sang Christmas songs, and I suppose there was some sort
of religious service, but I chiefly remember children recit-
ing poems or singing songs (the Hodges brothers did an
especially good "Santa Claus Is Coming To Town"). I remember, too, that the first electric Christmas tree lights I
ever saw were at this Christmas program.

The big event, though, was the arrival of Santa Claus.
For years I thought the pictures of Santa in a red coat were
all wrong. At Cassoday he wore a cowhide coat with black
hair on the outside (the very coat, in fact, that my grandfather wore at other times during the winter—it took me a
while to figure that one out). At any rate, Santa (usually
played by Ches Coffelt, janitor at the grade school and a
great favorite of all the kids) would come in ringing a set of
sleigh bells, laughing, and carrying a big white sack filled
with bags of candy, nuts, and oranges.

He would talk to the little kids, hand out the presents

under the tree (the ones that parents had brought in earlier), then distribute the candy in his sack before leaving. I learned only a few years ago, as did most people in town, that for years the candy was Deke Young's Christmas gift to the children of Cassoday (Deke was a local fixture, an old-time cowboy who had been injured years back when his horse fell).

We would go home then and hang up our stockings. Christmas was one morning we didn't mind getting up before Dad had built a fire in our wood stove, and we would go through our presents before going out to chore and feed the cows. Christmases are usually mild in our part of the plains (I even remember some years when the bees were out), but sometimes there is snow and lots of it. After the stock was fed and the ice broken, we would go to my grandparents for a day of eating, exchanging presents, and playing with the cousins.

Everyone has his own special Christmas memories, and they do seem to get stronger over the years. But even the meanest-hearted Scrooge should be allowed a little nostalgia about Christmas.—*JH*

60. *Recess Games*

For several years now, off and on, I have been collecting people's recollections of the games they played during recess at country schools. This may seem like an idle pursuit for a grown man, but I justify it on two counts. First, I am interested because I attended a country school of about ten pupils for two years until it was consolidated out of existence (the school was Pleasant Valley School, District 9, Barton County, Kansas). Second, I think these games tell us quite a bit about the shaping influences on generations of children, influences different from those affecting children now attending consolidated town schools.

Children in town schools today associate and play only

with children their own age. At recess, teachers supervise groups of pupils playing the organized sports common to American popular culture—soccer, softball, and so on. They have spacious playgrounds and ample equipment.

Contrast this with the situation in the country schools. There the children of all eight grades played together. Games had to be so designed that all ages of pupils could have active parts in them and still not dismember one another.

In the country schools teachers generally did not supervise play at recess. Most teachers had work to do during this time; some entered into games along with the children. In either case there was no referee. The players had to be self-governing.

Equipment was scarce. Children learned to do without or to use available objects (sticks, rocks, even the schoolhouse itself) as part of their games.

All this meant that instead of existing in an illusory world where everyone is the same age, pupils in the country schools became accustomed to competition and cooperation with comrades of various ages. In settling their own disputes, they learned basic fairness—not that fairness always ruled, but they recognized it even when it was violated. And they learned to improvise in the absence of resources.

More particularly, the games played were different in basic ways from games such as football or baseball. In football there are two teams, and one defeats the other. Such was the case also with some of the recess games, but not with most of them. More commonly the winning parties absorbed the losing ones rather than defeating them.

"Fox and Geese" was a good example of this and was one of the more picturesque recess games. This game required new-fallen snow, which the players tramped down into a pattern resembling a wheel with hub and four spokes. Most of the players were designated "geese" and congregated in the hub. One was called the "fox" and roamed about the spokes and rim of the snow-packed wheel. The

idea was for the geese to run from the hub out one of
the spokes, around the rim, and back through another
of the spokes to the hub, the fox in pursuit. If the fox
caught the goose, then the goose became another fox, and
so on until all were caught.

The point is that there was no winning team or even
any individual winner, unless the last goose caught could
be considered the winner. Instead, the object was to make
everyone a fox, and all players participated until the end.

In further chapters I intend to describe some other
common recess games of country schools on the plains. My
versions may differ a bit from yours, but in the aggregate,
these games represent one of the great commonalities of
culture on the plains.—*TI*

61. *"Dare Base"*

ONE of the problems with studying country-school recess
games is that it is difficult—at least for me—to summarize
the rules of the games. They seem to have been absorbed
and understood rather than stated and observed. And
some of the games were pretty complicated.

"Dare Base," for example. I find it easier to pitch in and
play this game with children than to explain it in the ab-
stract. "Dare Base," sometimes called "Prisoner's Base," was
one of the most common, widespread, and fun recess
games played on the plains. I have reports of it from Texas
to Saskatchewan.

The gist of the accounts as to how "Dare Base" was
played is like this. The players chose sides. Each side then
designated a home base, an area large enough to accommodate the entire team. The two home bases might be located eighty or a hundred feet apart.

Next, each side marked a prisoner's base, or stink base.
The stink base would be located off to the side of the
home base.

Each side also established a dare base, a spot situated a short distance in front of the home base. There were altogether too many bases in this game; that's one of the things that make it so confusing.

To begin the game, a player from one team coyly approached the dare base of the other team. He finally touched the dare base, whereupon he ran back toward his home base, players from the other team in pursuit, attempting to capture him by slapping him on the back. If they caught him, they took him to their stink base. He had to stay there.

That was simple enough. The complication was that any player who left his home base could be pursued in turn by a player from the other side. The rule was that any player who left his home base could be captured by a member of the other team who had left his home base at a later moment.

One more complication. Players could free teammates stranded on the other team's stink base by touching them. Of course, players attempting to liberate their comrades from the stink base were liable to be caught by opposing players who subsequently left their home base.

Several distinctive aspects of this game are obvious. First, it emphasized cooperation. Team members rescued one another from the stink base. The rescuer had to risk his own status for a teammate; the prisoner had to concede his own helplessness and await aid from a comrade.

Second, there were laurels to be won. The player who freed a number of teammates from the stink base was the hero of the moment.

Third, the game was full of strategy. As the action unfolded, team members decided among themselves who would pursue members of the other team, who would stand watch over prisoners, and who would attempt to liberate captured teammates. These arrangements had to be adjusted as more people were captured or freed.

And finally, "Dare Base" was a game rife with dispute. The great point of contention was the provision that the player who left home base later was eligible to capture an opposing player who left home base earlier. It was hard to keep track of who left home base when. Arguments were frequent and punctuated with the cry, "I had the base on you!"

The Duke of Wellington is reported to have said, "The Battle of Waterloo was won on the playing fields of Eton." If, as he implied, childhood games were preparation for later achievement, then "Dare Base" was at least part of the preparation for the accomplishments of people from the plains.—*TI*

62. *Sounds of the School Yard*

SOMETIMES it occurs to me that historians of the plains such as I have left a gap in our efforts to reconstruct the experiences of our forebears. We narrate what we think are the important events, and we describe the scenes that appear in our minds' eyes, but often we neglect the aural heritage of the region. What were the sounds of the past, and how were they different from those we are accustomed to today?

This thought occurred to me as I wrote about country-school recess games. Several of the games played on the plains incorporated distinct slogans or shouts as elements of the play. These sounds of the past rarely resound today.

"Annie Over!" was a cry with import to thousands of children, although some of them said it "Auntie Over," "Andy Over," or even "Handy Over." It meant that the kids on the other side of the schoolhouse should expect a ball to come over the roof, setting off a new round of pursuit by one team or the other. If the throw failed to clear the gable, the cry was "Pigtail!"

Likewise, most any pupil at a country school knew that the rhythmic chant, "Red Rover, Red Rover, send [insert name of one of the players] right over!" would bring a member of one team running headlong toward the human chain of the other team.

"Pom Pom Pullaway" was another game that used a slogan. This game required two bases; the schoolhouse generally was one, and a fence often was the other. One person was designated "it," and the rest went to the bases. They were to run back and forth between the bases while the it person tried to catch them. Anyone caught also became it. Should some timid player remain too long on base, then the its shouted, "Pom Pom Pullaway, if you don't come, I'll pull you away."

The most intricate of all the chants, though, was found in the game, "New York and Boston." The game began with two sides designating their home bases. One team then approached the other and began the chant, trading lines with the other team:

"Here we come!"

"Where you from?"

"New York" (or "Boston").

"What's your trade?"

"Lemonade."

"Show us some if you're not afraid."

Then the team that had begun the dialogue began to act out in pantomime an occupation, an animal, or whatever it was they wanted the other team to guess. When the other side guessed it, they shouted it out and chased the actors. Anyone they caught became a member of their own team. Sometimes, after the initial dialogue, the game continued much like dare base.

"New York and Boston" incorporated both mental creativity and physical activity. In fact, so did much of the country-school experience. Nostalgia aside, it had its good points.—*TI*

63. *Indoor School Games*

Tom has written quite a bit about outdoor recess games, stirring up many of my own school-day memories. Some of these memories are about games we played inside the schoolhouse. Some were recess games (on rainy days or during blizzards), but we also played during class time on the day before a holiday or other times at night while our parents were meeting in another room.

I'm sure there were other games, but the ones I remember playing most were "Button, Button, Who's Got the Button," "Fruit Basket," "Mother, May I?" and "Gossip." I have pretty much forgotten the rules of the first one, but I still remember how to play the others.

In "Button, Button" I recall that someone (it seemed like it was always a girl who got to do it) would go around with a button between her cupped hands, pretending to drop it into the also-cupped hands of several children seated in a circle. One would actually receive the button, then someone would say "Button, button, who's got the button?" What happened next I don't remember. Maybe that's because I never got the button.

In "Fruit Basket" I remember that two children would be apples, two pears, two bananas, etc. At a signal of some sort, the two apples would exchange seats. I think that, like "Musical Chairs," the object was for the It person to try to get a seat. The big excitement came when someone called "fruit basket upset," and everybody had to change seats.

Everyone, I think, has played "Gossip," a game still current. The first child whispers something to the second, who whispers what he heard (which usually is not what was actually said) to the next, and so on around the room. The end result, of course, is far different from the original secret, from which the fun of the game arises.

I'm not really sure about the hidden agenda of the other games, but "Mother May I?" taught a definite moral lesson. All the players but one (the It or Mother) lined up on one wall, the object being to cross to the other side first—but only according to Mother's orders.

"Jim, you may take two scissor steps forward and one baby step back." "Mother, may I?" "Yes, you may." And I had made some progress. Not as much as if I had been permitted five giant (or elephant) steps forward, or even three regular steps, but much more than just a couple of baby steps (the length of one's foot) or if I had been told to take all my steps backward.

But if one forgot to ask permission, it was back to the starting line. Immediately, without question. No quarter granted, though often pleaded.

Obviously, this game teaches about real life. For one thing, you shouldn't question your mother's orders: "You *will* eat your peas, or you'll get no dessert!" More pragmatically, it teaches the importance of following the forms of courtesy. Politeness, even if not totally sincere, will help speed one along in life.

Then there was the version we played on our own, one not condoned by the teacher. Here cheating was permissible, although usually practiced by only a few and always under great protest by the other participants. When Mother's attention was elsewhere, you could sneak forward. But if you were caught, it was back to the starting line.

The ethics were questionable, to say the least, but certainly not unknown in the world beyond the schoolroom.—*JH*

64.   *Reprise of the Recess Games*

LETTERS from readers, as well as expressions by some of my summer folklore students, show broad enthusiasm for the subject of country-school recess games. Maybe my interest in this topic is not so eccentric, after all.

Now the problem I have is that the more information I collect, the more complicated it gets. For instance, a number of people have insisted to me that the game I call "New York and Boston" is not that at all, but rather one they call "New Orleans." These seem to be just variant names for the same basic game, however.

Names for games can take some peculiar turns. For example, I thought that everyone, as I did, referred to the game in which kids threw a ball over the schoolhouse as "Annie Over," but not so. Some players conferred male gender on the contest and called it "Andy Over." Still others gave it a utilitarian ring by terming it "Handy Over." I'm not sure what to think about another variant name reported to me by several people—"Anti Over." Might this be a product of the Cold War and nuclear age? No, I think rather that the original usage was "Auntie Over," and my youthful field collectors have conferred upon the term its strategic spelling.

This "Anti Over" business raises the general issue of interference by mass-media popular culture in the traditional folkways of the school yard. This was already going on generations ago. Thinking back on my own experiences, and talking to other people who went to country schools, I find that although we might have played traditional games, we also felt compelled to join in the team sports common to American popular culture.

The problem was that in the country schools there might be too few players for such sports as baseball or football. In baseball the answer to this problem was "Work-Up," a game, common to both urban and rural settings, in which there were no set teams and in which individual players took turns batting and playing the various positions in the field.

I am more interested in a football adaptation that I recall from my youth; I have found only a few people scattered around the region who are familiar with it. It was called "Three-Step." This game began with the kids choosing up sides and designating two goal lines. A good player from one team then kicked off to the other team with either a place kick or a punt.

If a member of the other team caught the ball on the fly, then he got to take three steps forward before punting it back toward the other goal. If he fumbled, he had to punt from where he touched the ball. The object of the game was for one team to punt the ball so deep behind the other team's goal line that they could not punt it back out again.

What made this game true folklore was that it underwent variations. Someone—probably someone leery of catching high punts on the fly—came up with the idea that if you caught the ball on the first bounce, then you could take one step forward before punting. A major change in the game came with a new rule—if you can call such things "rules"—that when you caught the ball on the fly, you could mark the spot of the catch with a line of dirt, back up for a running start, and take your three steps in a triple jump before punting. In doing this, of course, you gave up the element of surprise whereby you might punt the ball in a place where no one, or perhaps just a lowly second-grader, was there to catch it. On the other hand, three running steps advanced the ball a long way.

This triple-jump deal was to the detriment of the game. It made long-legged eighth-graders too important in relation to the other players, and Lord knows, the eighth-graders thought they were mighty important anyway.—*TI*

Part Six

FARM AND RANCH

I<small>F</small>, as I said earlier, the sounds of the plains are a neglected feature of the region's heritage, then no historical sound is more deserving of attention than the steam whistle. The age of steam on farms of the Great Plains was from the 1880s to the 1920s. Although applicable to other farm operations, steam engines were most useful for threshing.

"How I still remember how the steam whistle sounded," recalls Guy Bretz, a present-day resident of Missouri who grew up in Lane County, Kansas. "You could hear it for a mile on still days. One to stop—two to start—three for water, and four for wheat wagons." As Bretz indicates, steam threshing outfits had definite codes of steam whistle signals given by the engineer.

Two other old threshermen—William Lies, of New Rockford, North Dakota, and Ted Worrall, of Loma, Montana—have sent me lists of whistle signals that they remember governed their outfits. According to Lies, if the engineer for any reason wanted the pitchers to stop pitching into the separator, he gave one short peep. Two short ones meant to start pitching again. If he was running low on water, he gave three long blasts. If the grain wagon was getting full, he signaled with two long blasts for the haulers to hurry with another wagon. Three short toots told the bundle-wagon drivers to hustle in from the field with more bundles. One long blast meant quitting time.

"Then there was the one that used to send a tingle down my back," Lies recalls. "That was when we heard four long blasts, which meant the boss was wanted for some reason or another."

The signals remembered by Worrall—or really by a friend of his named Al Herman—went like this. The engineer gave one long blast at a number of times during the day—one-half hour before starting time, for dinner at noon, after dinner at one, at the end of the set, and at the end of a job. Two short toots meant the engineer was about to set the machinery in motion. Three short toots meant to hurry with the bundle wagons. To signal the water monkey, the engineer gave two rather long blasts interspersed with one short one. A rapid series of short peeps meant some mechanical difficulty, such as a belt off or the blower plugged. Five long blasts indicated serious trouble, such as an injury or a fire.

Some of Worrall's signals agree with those of Lies, and others do not. I suspect that if I compiled recollections on the subject from old-timers all over the plains, certain signals would prove to have been nearly universal, while others would prove typical only of particular outfits or localities. I'd be happy to hear from old threshermen, pitchers, and farmers who recall whistle signals they used.

I'm sure there was a time also for some childish mischief with the whistle. "We young fellows got a hand on it, too," says George Hitz of his childhood in North Dakota, "pulling the whistle string when they pulled the outfit in from the field to the yard when they had finished a run till the pressure in the boiler diminished to the point that the whistle was so weak that it wasn't interesting anymore." At the end of the run, a little horseplay with the whistle was pardonable.—*TI*

66. *Wooden Silos*

SILOS never have been such a dominant part of the landscape of the Great Plains as they have been in the corn-hog-cattle-dairy belt of the Midwest, but the plains do contain quite a variety of these useful structures. The advent of silos in this region marked a change from the feeding of feed grains for fattening stock to the feeding of silage, usually made from sorgo cane, sometimes from corn.

Some farmers on the plains erected concrete, metal, or tile silos just as substantial as those farther east, but the tendency out West was to cut down the capital investment by designing less expensive alternatives. Some farmers stacked up hay bales to form a silo. Others wrapped lath snow fence in a circle; this was sometimes called a "corn-slat silo." The most satisfactory, inexpensive style, though, was the trench silo, which was best located on a hillside. This was the kind of silo that I was accustomed to in my youth and that has become increasingly prevalent in recent years.

That's why I was surprised to discover, about six miles northeast of Hamilton, Kansas, a substantial silo constructed entirely of wood. It has ten sides and sits on a concrete foundation. The side walls are composed of two-by-sixes and two-by-fours about six feet long.

The boards sit flat, stacked one upon another, the corners cut in such a way that the end of one board overlaps the end of the previous layer on the adjacent wall. No construction nails show inside or out; all were driven from above into the layer of boards below.

The lower part of the silo is made of two-by-sixes. I counted 107 layers up from the bottom, which comes to better than seventeen feet. The upper part is constructed of two-by-fours. I counted 100 layers of these, which figures up more than sixteen feet. So the structure stands a little more than thirty-four feet tall.

Apparently the inside of the silo was lined partway up with tar paper; there are tar-paper nails and bits of paper still clinging to the inside walls. On the southwest side of the silo are six windows for blowing in or loading out silage; a ladder of two-inch lumber runs up the windows.

Some old-timers around Hamilton say that there used to be many wooden silos in the area, but that this is the only one remaining. The present owner, Dr. Olen Stauffer, lives in Yates Center, Kansas. He says that the silo was built by the Cotrall family in 1903 with lumber salvaged from two older wooden silos that blew down in a tornado. By his recollection, the silo was last filled, with corn, in 1939. Still, it stands today in good shape. Only a few small bits are splintering off the wallboards.

This is the only wooden silo I have encountered. Arn Henderson, a professor of architecture at the University of Oklahoma, who has done considerable fieldwork on the folk architecture of the southern plains, says he has seen one other like it, in southeastern Colorado.

If wooden silos were numerous in earlier times, but few stand today, then they must have been more vulnerable to wear and disaster than silos of other materials. Obviously, they were more subject to destruction by wind or fire; perhaps spontaneous combustion of heating silage destroyed them.—*TI*

67. *More About Wooden Silos*

RESPONSE to an essay about wooden silos on the plains sent me to the government document stacks for research on methods of construction. The old USDA *Farmer's Bulletin*s I found describe two main types of wooden silos—wood-stave and timber-crib. Readers have sent me information about both types on the plains.

Mrs. S. Wesley Jensen, a former resident of Marion County, Kansas, now living in California, mailed me some photographs that belong to her mother, Eulah Riggs. One of them, dating from about 1911, shows a group of Marion County men erecting a wood-stave silo. In a wood-stave silo the boards stand vertical and usually are fit together in a tongue-and-groove arrangement. The men in the photograph are ascending and descending with blocks and tackles, instead of using the more common scaffolding. Eulah's husband, Harry M. Riggs, sold the staves out of a hardware store in Marion.

The wood-stave salesmen must have been pretty busy around Marion. According to a recent notice in the *Marion County Record,* quite a few farmers in the vicinity erected wood-stave silos before World War I. One of them still stands on "the old Pete Goentzel place" southwest of town.

Wood-stave silos also were used in northwest Texas, according to some material from T. Lindsay Baker, of the Panhandle-Plains Historical Museum, in Canyon, Texas. He sent me a photograph of a crew filling a wood-stave silo near Friona, Texas. The silo is brand-new; it has no roof yet, and the scaffolding is still standing around it.

What was the most interesting in the material Lindsay sent me, however, was a photograph of another crew filling a timber-crib silo on the Fred Hettler farm, near Lubbock, Texas, in 1916. At least it looks like a timber-crib silo. In a timber-crib silo, the main boards of construction, generally two-by-fours, lie flat and horizontal, stacked upon one another to raise the walls. This is the type of structure I found near Hamilton, Kansas, and wrote about in the earlier wooden silo chapter. The octagonal silo in the Lubbock photograph appears to have been sided with vertical boards outside the horizontal timbers, a procedure recommended by agricultural bulletins of the day.

I eventually brought this quest for wooden silos to a climax with an inspection of another timber-crib silo that still stands a few miles northeast of Burdick, Kansas. Mrs. Wendell Peterson, postmistress of Burdick, guided me to the site, the farmstead residence of eighty-four-year-old Blanche Huyler.

This silo stands 220 flat two-by-fours high and is capped by a wood-shingle gambrel roof. The timbers are in good shape, but the whole structure is leaning. Atop it protrude the shattered remains of a flagpole. Blanche says the original owner, a dairyman named Walter Stevens, "was very patriotic."

The silo last held silage in about 1941. Occasional users since then have stored oats, ear corn, or hay in it.

Although I doubt that wooden silos ever were as common on the plains as those of concrete or tile, they evidently were widely used. One reason for their present scarcity may be their material of construction: good lumber is too valuable to leave standing in an unused silo.—TI

68.   *Used Tires*

WHAT do you do with your old, worn-out tires? Many plains dwellers put them to continued use, getting as much good out of them off the car (or truck or tractor) as on.

One use, shared with city dwellers, is recreational: swings for children. Fancier ones have much of the tire body cut away, leaving only the two circular beads and about one-fourth of the tread. This is then turned inside out and hung from a tree. The simpler method is to tie a rope or chain around the tire and hang it up. Optimists will cut a hole in the bottom to let the rainwater drain out. And cautious people will always give a strange tire swing a good, sharp rap before climbing in; wasps like them as much as children do.

Old tires also make good livestock feeders. My father makes oat feeders for calves or horses by cutting one bead off a used tire, then turning it inside out and nailing it to a wooden platform. The platform is nailed to a pair of two-by-fours to hold it off the ground. This feeder also makes a nice, noncorrodable holder for block salt.

My horses eat hay out of feeders made of tractor tires stacked up and laced together with baling wire. One feeder is three tires deep and holds a loosened bale easily, while the two-tire feeder is a handier height for the kids to tip a bale into, leaving the wires on it.

Many farmers throughout the plains region cover their filled trench silos with plastic, then cover the plastic solidly with tires to protect it from wind. The same ploy works for haystacks as well. Near Council Grove, Kansas, I have seen some of the big round bales placed on truck or tractor tires to keep the bottoms from rotting away.

Recently, while driving through the Sandhills near Arthur, Nebraska, I saw in the distance a double row of tires running parallel down the side of a hill. As I drew nearer, I could see that a fence ran between the two rows. A few miles later I noticed that each pole of an electric highline had four tires encircling its base. Corner posts also had old tires surrounding them, and I have seen posts in western Kansas with a tire dropped over them before the wire was strung. Wind erosion, of course, is a constant threat in the sandy areas of the Great Plains, and these tires were helping to keep the shifting sand in place. I suppose, also, that the double row of tires along the Sandhills fence not only helped to keep the posts in the ground, but also kept the cow paths from becoming too deep and turning into miniature Grand Canyons.

Nebraskans and Wyoming residents seem to favor old truck and tractor tires for cattle-guard wings, an effective but not too pretty substitute for the pipe or rod triangle usually found connecting grid to fence. One South Dakota rancher has made an entire cattle guard by bolting a dozen or so tires together in three rows. Passenger cars can't cross it, but pickups and feed trucks can. The cowboy who told me about it said that it sure kept the pheasant hunters out.

Nearly as unusual as the tire cattle guard is the windbreak made of stacked tires I saw in the Sandhills. It must have been six feet high and over twenty yards long, the ends curved toward the south. I must admit that most old tires (and things made of them) are not very pretty to look at, but this windbreak had a kind of charm—almost like the turrets of a medieval castle.

Attractive or not, the structures and devices made of old tires are physical proof of the ingenuity—and the thriftiness—of Great Plains farmers and ranchers.—*JH*

69. *Mailboxes*

A FAVORITE TOPIC for folklorists is the rural mailbox, probably because the creativity displayed in unusual mailboxes is a prime example of the folk urge to express individuality or to boast of one's occupation, while simultaneously beautifying a utilitarian object.

Oilmen, for example, often mount their mailboxes on miniature derricks or pump jacks, or on old drilling bits, just as farmers will use an antique implement (often a plow or lister) as a holder. Dairymen incline toward ten-gallon milk cans to anchor mailbox posts, or they will set the box on a cream separator.

Sometimes the posts themselves are of unusual materials—a huge steel coil spring, for instance, or a tree trunk with one branch holding a mailbox and another a sign with the name of the farm or the owners. I have seen mailboxes in the Flint Hills and in the post-rock region of Kansas fixed atop stone posts.

Sandhills Nebraskans seem to be a particularly patriotic lot: many red, white, and blue mailboxes up there. Also in Nebraska I recall seeing the mailbox for an automotive repair shop attached to a V-8 engine, fan blades turning in the wind.

Farmers with welding outfits often make unusual mailbox holders—an iron-rod cowboy or cow or cattle brand. Sometimes the links in a large log chain will be spot-welded so that the chain curves up into the air, the mailbox attached to the hook at the end of the chain.

I have noticed in mountainous regions that mail is often deposited in barrels that swing freely from chains attached to tall poles set back away from the road. I have visited mountains only in the summers, but I am told that these mailboxes are built for winter conditions. Snowplows opening a road can hit a mailbox barrel without knocking it down or tearing it apart.

One of the more unusual mailbox arrangements I have seen is located in the Gypsum Hills of south-central Kansas. Much of this area is open-range country. I noticed, while driving some of these range roads, that many of the mailboxes were literally surrounded by wooden fence posts—a post in the back and a couple on each side. I snapped some photographs of these mailboxes, but remained puzzled as to their purpose until I saw another, more attractive arrangement.

This particular rancher had welded old harrow bars, teeth firmly in place, around the edges of his mailbox, with two bars slanted down from the ends of the box to the post that held it. The protruding teeth were the clue as to what was going on; they, and the posts on the other mailboxes, kept cattle from rubbing the mailbox down.

No real attempt at individuality or beautification was made in these Gypsum Hills mailboxes, but they were perfect examples of folk ingenuity in this region of the plains.—*JH*

70. *Pasture Burning*

NIGHTTIME DRIVERS through the Flint Hills of Kansas in late April often feel that they have driven into the end of the world. In all directions, skies glow orange with fire, and the air is filled with towering billows of sweet smoke. It's one of my favorite seasons in the hills—pasture-burning time.

While accidental fires (often started by lightning or sparks from locomotives) are almost invariably detrimental, the deliberate burning of pasturelands (and, for different reasons, of forests also) is now recognized by the scientific community as a sound conservation and range management tool—killing weeds and undesirable grasses, controlling trees and brush, helping to ensure even grazing.

As is often the case, folk wisdom has preceded scientific knowledge. Flint Hills ranchers have been practicing spring burning for nearly a century, and from Texas to Montana the Plains Indians had burned the prairies from time immemorial in order to attract bison to the new growth of grass that followed a fire. From around 1930 to the mid-1970s, however, extensive and deliberate pasture burning occurred only in the Flint Hills. Today ranchers in the rest of Kansas and other states as well are reviving the practice.

The Flint Hills have traditionally been used for the fattening of Texas cattle. Many early-day Texas ranchers insisted that the pastures be burned yearly so that their steers would have an easy access to newgrowth bluestem, the high-protein grass that could double the weight of an aged steer in only three or four months. So Flint Hills ranchers, at the behest of the Texans, tended to burn in March, not, as today, in April and May, when weeds and brush can more easily be killed (which proves that scientific knowledge is sometimes superior to folk wisdom).

Pasture burning is often a communal effort, neighbor helping neighbor, both for the sharing of work and for the protection of one's own property. I remember using a pitchfork to scrape up some dead grass, setting it afire, then stringing it along to set either back- or headfires. I also remember beating out flames with gunnysacks that had been wetted in barrels of water. Sometime in the fifties, though, the mechanized cattle sprayer became available and the managing of intentional prairie fires became much easier, as did the fighting of accidental fires.

Conditions need to be right for burning—not too windy or the fire can get out of control, but windy enough so that the headfire will move quickly over the prairie. Wooden fence posts are especially vulnerable to slow fire (although I know of some hedge posts that have been resisting both fire and rotting for most of this century).

Wind is definitely the big variable in pasture burning. A change in either speed or direction can cause instant trouble. Smoldering cow chips are another problem. The flames of a prairie fire can be entirely gone, but a gust of wind can stir sparks out of a cow chip, carrying them into unburned grass and rekindling a blaze.

One folk belief states that rain will not put out a fire started by lightning. I don't know how scientifically valid that belief is, but I do know that some of the worst fires I ever helped fight were caused by summer storms.—*JH*

71. *Russian Thistles*

Do you ever attempt to reconstruct through your mind's eye the primeval landscape of the plains, to imagine the region as it was before white men entered it? I do, and it's more complicated than it seems, because so many of the plants that we consider characteristic of the North American plains are not native to them but were introduced by immigrant farmers.

Consider the Russian thistle, a common tumbleweed generally classified a noxious weed. Stories as to the specifics of how the Russian thistle came to the American plains vary, but evidently it traveled to the area with flaxseed carried from Russia by German-Russian immigrants during the late 1870s. (Some say the German-Russians purposely sowed the seed in the fields of local enemies, but this tale sounds like the product of embittered, jealous neighbors.)

The thistle, moving easily from the steppes of Russia to the plains of the United States, thrived in the Dakotas. Because of its habit of breaking off and tumbling in the wind, it also spread quickly to the north and south. Its rapid establishment prompted a study in 1893 by the U.S. Department of Agriculture, the author of which, L. H. Dewey, concluded that the thistles "seem to have partaken of the conquering spirit of the West."

Early researchers such as Dewey developed a love-hate relationship with the new weed. Ada A. Georgia, writing for one of the Bailey Rural Manuals in 1915, called it "a most pernicious weed," but also described with wonder the transformation that the plant exhibited during its life cycle—how it progressed from "innocent-looking, grass-like shoots" to "tender and succulent stalks" that "cattle and sheep eat greedily." Then the tender leaves fell away and were replaced by short, awl-like spines; the stem turned woody and red; and the plant branched and spread to choke out other growth.

Farmers harbored no scientific fascination to temper their hatred of the thistle. It invaded and sapped the moisture from their fields. Its spines lacerated the legs of horses and broke off to cause festering sores. Threshers also cursed the spines, which penetrated the best gloves. The tough stalks broke sickles on mowers and harvesting machines. The tumbleweeds piled up against fences and even were blamed for the spread of prairie fires.

Unlike such weeds as bindweed, the Russian thistle at

least could be checked through cultivation, burning, and other cultural controls. The thistle survived decades of war against it, though, here and there emerging to remind the thoughtless husbandman that his cultivation was inadequate or his grazing practices too intensive.

It was fortunate that the thistle did survive until the 1930s and 1950s, for during those times it proved a blessing, as two great grassland ecologists, J. E. Weaver, of Nebraska, and F. W. Albertson, of the Fort Hays Kansas State Experiment Station, pointed out in *Grasslands of the Great Plains*. When blowing dirt buried cropland or denuded rangeland, the first annual weed to reoccupy the ravaged ground and stabilize it was the Russian thistle. "This species alone or almost alone covered hundreds of square miles of the dust bowl," Weaver and Albertson observed. The Russian thistle was a necessary stage in the succession back toward stable grassland. Its young plants often also provided the only grazing available and even were consumed by humans as a green vegetable.

Is there any plant or animal that is truly an unmixed blessing or curse?—*TI*

72.   *Frank Meyer and the Chinese Elm*

PEOPLE on the plains are great tree planters. They may love their open horizons and their red sunsets, but around the homeplace they are determined to have shade and windbreaks. Unfortunately, the semiarid plains are not the best environment for most trees.

That's why I'm tired of outsiders belittling the types of trees that do well on the plains—the Osage orange, the cottonwood, the mesquite, the Russian olive, and, especially, the Chinese elm. The old Chinese elm may not be particularly graceful, it may lose its limbs in storms, it may be full of beetles, and it may scatter its seeds everywhere, but it grows fast and shelters tens of thousands of farmsteads, not to mention villages and towns.

How much less hospitable the plains would be if a strange set of circumstances had not led to the introduction of this tree from Asia. The story began in 1905 when a Dutch botanist, named Frank Meyer, went to work for the U.S. Department of Agriculture as a plant explorer. Plant explorers were special agents of the USDA who searched overseas for plants of use to American farmers.

A major concern of officials of the plant-exploration program was to find plants suitable for the American plains. So they sent explorers to other dry, tree-poor regions of the world to find hardy new species to introduce into the United States.

From 1905 to 1918 Meyer made four expeditions to China and other parts of the Far East. He was a tireless explorer, equally able to stand off anti-American mobs, endure ever-present vermin, and cross a continent on foot. "I have strong calves and love to walk," he explained simply.

Meyer was successful both because of his botanical expertise and because of his restless disposition, which continually led him farther afield. "A man is constantly wishing and longing for farther off and unseen places," he mused. "Why do we have that desire?"

That desire, whatever its source, took Meyer to Manchuria, where he discovered a remarkable elm tree, "which in its native haunts resists drought and alkali to a considerable degree," he noted, and "proves to be of remarkable vigor and of great promise as a shade tree and windbreak in the Upper Mississippi Valley, where shade trees have a hard struggle with the climate."

This prize was the Chinese (later called Siberian) elm, destined to play a major role in the forestation of the American plains. Tough plant that it was, it survived shipment to the United States to be distributed broadly by the USDA and then to spread on its own. Meyer made thousands of other discoveries and introductions, but no other was of such environmental importance to the plains.

Yet poor Meyer died unhappily in 1918. The tragic aspect of his career was that the same driving spirit that propelled him to distinction also brought him unbearable loneliness. The outbreak of World War I caused him such despair that finally he leaped from the deck of a Japanese steamer and drowned in the Yangtze River.

Meyer's body is buried in Shanghai, but his leafy memorial sways forever with the winds of the plains.—*TI*

73. *Mark Carleton, Plant Explorer*

IN an earlier chapter I said that the Great Plains was one region the plant explorers particularly sought plants for. What I didn't mention was that one of the greatest of all plant explorers was a Kansan named Mark Carleton.

Carleton was a farm boy from near Concordia, Kansas, and a graduate of Kansas Agricultural College, Manhattan. Although he became an eminent botanist, he was regarded as an odd duck in the scientific pond. His colleagues clucked their tongues at his unkempt clothing, abrupt speech, bushy moustache, and general awkwardness. "Carleton went at everything like he was driving cattle," one of them said.

Underneath the rough exterior there hummed an agile mind with the quality that sets the genius apart from the plodding executor of experiments—the creative ability to see veiled connections between diverse phenomena. This quality showed itself during the early 1890s, when Carleton solved the mystery of how that destructive fungus, the black stem rust, infested fields of wheat across the plains. By figuring out the life history of the rust, he learned that the villain behind the infestation was the barberry bush, an alternate host of the fungus.

That discovery may not seem too exciting, but Carleton's mind was capable of much broader and more romantic leaps. He moved from investigation of grain rusts to research on all manner of pests and problems associated with wheat farming, especially the question of raising wheat on the semiarid high plains.

Carleton decided that the wheat varities then raised in

the United States were too frail to stand up to plague and drought. From that premise he proceeded to a hypothesis that carved a new path down which others would follow: he speculated that the place to find wheats suitable for the American plains was in the flat, semiarid regions of other continents, where thousands of years of natural and intentional selection would have produced the wheats best suited to conditions.

If this seems obvious now, it was not so then; the idea that environment shaped the evolution of a plant, although commonplace in theory, was new to the applied science of agriculture.

That idea took Carleton to Czarist Russia in 1898 and again in 1900 as a plant explorer. He grumbled at bureaucratic delays, struggled with strange dialects, and suffered the hardships of overland travel on the vast steppes, but he returned with rare prizes.

For the northern plains, Carleton discovered Kubanka durum wheat. It was too hard to mill, and its flour baked poorly, but it was perfectly resistant to black stem rust and made delicious pasta. Hence the birth of the spring durum wheat industry still so important in the Dakotas.

For the southern plains, he brought back Kharkov, a hard red winter wheat. Although German-Russian Mennonites deserve credit as early pioneers of hard red winter wheat farming on the plains, it was Carleton and his followers who accomplished the broad dissemination and acceptance of the crop. Scientists and seedmen repeatedly followed Carleton to Russia for more hard red wheats, the progenitors of modern productive varieties.

Not bad for a clumsy cattle driver from Concordia.—*TI*

74. *Circles*

IF there is an artist somewhere looking for a graphic symbol of contemporary life on the Great Plains, then I think he or she ought to consider the center-pivot irrigation sys-

tem, or "circle," as people on the plains generally call it.
One reason is that circles have a powerful aesthetic appeal.
Standing idle in the field, their lines are wonderfully stark.
In operation on a sunny day, they create multiple rainbows
as sunlight embraces the descending droplets of water.
Viewed from an airplane, they form a remarkable pattern,
like green checkers on a brown board.

Moreover, the center pivot both originated and found
its greatest use on the plains.

The inventor of the center pivot was Frank Zybach, a
resident of Columbus, Nebraska, who during the late 1940s
was dryland farming near Strasburg, Colorado. After attending an irrigation field day, he came away convinced
that there must be some way to cut down the amount of
labor necessary for sprinkler irrigation. His thinking and
tinkering resulted, in 1949, in a patent application for the
"Zybach Self-Propelled Sprinkler Irrigation Apparatus."

By the time the patent was conferred in 1952, Zybach
had built a prototype circle and installed it on the Ernest
Englebrecht farm, near Strasburg, to irrigate forty acres of
alfalfa. Receiving the patent, Zybach took in a partner,
A. E. Trowbridge, an automobile dealer in Columbus. During the next year or so they manufactured ten circles in a
rented machine shop in Columbus.

In 1954 Zybach and Trowbridge sold exclusive manufacturing rights to Valley Manufacturing Company, of Valley, Nebraska. The two developers received a royalty on
every circle manufactured by Valley (which changed its
name to Valmont Industries in 1967) until the patent ran
out in 1969. Since then at least thirty firms have entered
the circle-manufacturing business, with Lindsay Manufacturing, of Lindsay, Nebraska, emerging as the largest com-
petitor to Valmont.

The circle found its home on the Great Plains. In most
parts of the plains, if ground water was available, circles
could be installed without much clearing. Circles incorporated the major advantage of sprinkler irrigation in that
they could be used on ground too uneven for flood irriga-

tion. But they eliminated the hand labor involved with the operation of previous sprinkler systems. Anyone who has stumbled through a field of beans carrying sprinkler pipe, or perhaps hefted the pipe above his head in order to move it across a field of corn or atlas, appreciates this.

It's difficult to get estimates of the number of circles in use on the plains, but according to Richard Black, an irrigation engineer with the state extension service, nearly ten thousand are plying Kansas. Nebraska undoubtedly has more, Texas, Colorado, and other states of the plains somewhat fewer.

It seems that most of the great advances of technology implemented on the plains were importations from elsewhere, but the circle is an example of one that originated here and was exported to benefit other regions.—*TI*

75. *Fraud on the Farm*

"A STUDENT of the social history of the American farmer in the late nineteenth century must be impressed by the infinite variety of humbugs developed to cheat rural people"— so says historian Earl Hayter in a fine book, *The Troubled Farmer*. The book is about how farmers in the United States struggled to adjust to the growth of industrial and urban society. One section deals with the many frauds perpetrated against farmers by nineteenth-century peddlers of trees, vegetable seeds, incubators, and, of course, lightning rods.

On the water-poor plains there was special opportunity for swindlers who specialized in water. Pluviculturalists (rainmakers) and water witches plied their trades profitably. And if the old county-agent reports I have been reading are any indication, fraud on the farm continued rampant well into the twentieth century.

County agents, considering themselves purveyors of reliable, scientific advice, were concerned about the activities of swindlers. They were especially concerned when some peddler made his pitch on the basis of agricultural improvement, thereby discrediting legitimate scientific advance.

For instance, county agents in the 1920s and 1930s spent a lot of time teaching keepers of chickens that they should cull diseased birds and poor layers from their flocks each summer. An enterprising fellow from Denver took his cue from this and began working farms in neighboring states. He would come to the farm and announce that he represented the "State Poultry Association," was working with the local county agent, and had come to cull the flock. Upon examining the birds, he announced with alarm that they were infested with some fearful disease or vermin. Fortunately, he happened to have in his automobile a supply of liquid remedy that would clear up the problem, which he sold for twelve dollars a gallon.

Or there was the livestock-improvement scam. During the 1930s agents traveling the region claimed to represent a "livestock-improvement association." One persuaded farmers to buy fine Chester White sows for $150 each with the promise that the association would buy back gilt offspring of the sow for $75 each. This sounded fine, but there were a couple of strings. For the association to buy the gilts, the farmer had to have the sow bred to a boar provided by the association, which charged a fee for the service. More telling yet was the simple economic logic of the situation. The bogus association might indeed buy some gilts for $75, but it could do so only as long as it continued to sell sows for $150. The true market worth of the sows was only about $30. Consequently, the livestock-improvement agent generally disappeared after a short time in the locality.

My cousin Bernice says her grandmother knew how to handle this sort of character. Of German descent and bilingual, she dismissed most peddlers by disclaiming knowledge of English. There was one particularly persistent fellow, though, who was selling a wonderful bottled medicine.

At the height of his pitch he rattled off a list of all the
things the stuff could cure, everything from gout to the va-
pors. When he paused for breath, she just announced, "I
don't got none of that schtuff," and slammed the door on
him.—*TI*

76. Farm Sales

IN any rural community a farm sale is always an important
occasion. Sometimes that occasion can be sad (when the
farm is being sold because of the death of the owner, or the
family has not been able to make a go of farming), sometimes it can be happier (when the family is leaving because
it wants to), but a farm sale is always exciting. The big machinery never held much attraction for me, but I loved to
walk around the wagons loaded with "junk" and look for
interesting items—old cow kickers, worn-out fence pliers,
bridle bits, maybe even a good pocket knife.

The food always tasted especially good at a farm sale,
maybe because most of the sales (or at least the ones we
went to) were held in the early spring or autumn, when the
weather was cool and crisp. Or rainy. In any case, when it
comes to taste, I would put a farm-sale hot dog up against a
baseball-game hot dog any day. And the pies—homemade
by the Ladies Aid Society or the Farm Bureau wives.

The first farm sale I remember going to was that of my
uncle, Marshall Hoy, who moved away from Cassoday in
1946. We still have a handbill from that sale—dated February 18—and it shows that he sold fourteen mules (including eight "Molly" mules, a common term for mare mules),
thirteen horses (including a team of work mares and five
bred mares—three to a jack and two to a quarter horse),
fifteen hogs, nineteen cattle, and a variety of farm machinery. There were no tractors and only one piece of tractor machinery, a two-bottom plow. There were, however,
three sets of harness, four mule collars, and a set of new

lines. Obviously horsepower had not yet come to an end in the Flint Hills.

The main thing I remember about that sale, though, is sharing a piece of pumpkin pie with my cousin, Judy. We were both six years old at the time, and we always got along well together, even though we tended to do things backwards from each other. I liked pie filling, she liked the crust. So that's how we ate it that day.

I don't remember the auctioneer, W. D. McIntosh, at my uncle's sale, nor do I remember Uncle Jim Hoy, who had quite a local reputation as an auctioneer, but I do remember several of the auctioneers in the area—Bob Jackson, from Chelsea; Jim Butts, from Leon; Jim Barr, from Cottonwood Falls. No matter how much money the merchandise brings, you can't have a good sale without a good auctioneer, at least from the spectator's point of view. Uncle Jim was supposed to be especially good, I am told, because he could play the crowd so well. If interest was lagging, he would tell a joke, and he was renowned as a storyteller, so people would stop their visiting and listen.

Not that there's anything wrong with visiting with your neighbors at a farm sale. That's one of the main reasons for going, along with seeing how much everything brings. Farm sales are great for kids—exploring strange barns, playing hide-and-seek in silos and haymows, meeting new dogs and cats.

They can also be educational. I remember the first time I ever bought anything at a sale. One of our neighbors was selling out and he had something I wanted very much—a goat. Goats were cheap back around 1950, and I think that I paid something like seventy-five cents for that one. And I could have had him for less if I hadn't kept bidding every time the auctioneer asked for another quarter. I had opened the bidding at a quarter and I had been the only bidder when the auctioneer stopped at seventy-five cents. I guess he took pity on me, or else he realized that no one else wanted the goat.

Mother wasn't too thrilled with my purchase, but we

kept the goat around for awhile, then Dad and I took him to the community sale in El Dorado. He actually made a little money, not counting feed and transportation costs.

After a farm sale is over comes the settling up with the clerk and loading up—putting boxes of miscellaneous junk into the trunk of the car or getting a neighbor to help load a piece of big machinery onto the back of the truck.

Almost invariably buyers at auctions think they have gotten bargains, and often they have. Usually, though, the seller as well comes out all right, and he has also provided a service—a place and an occasion for the community to come together.—*JH*

Part Seven

GOOD FENCES, GOOD NEIGHBORS

THE HOT WIRE, or electric fence, not only is an important tool for crop and livestock management but also has sparked (pretty good accidental pun) quite a bit of folk invention, both technological and literary. Anyone who has worked much with electric fences has hit upon a few tricks for saving time and steps in putting them up or taking them down. Anyone who has been around them much has a choice story about some hapless person's (or animal's) experience with the hot wire.

When a new article of technology such as electric fencing comes along, it adds something to rural culture—"culture" meaning the accumulation of experiences we have in common. See if some of the following situations and dialogues don't seem familiar to you.

1. "Is that wire hot?" says the younger brother, told to take down the wire so some stock can cross.

"Touch it and see." Of course it is.

2. Elder brother and younger brother go out to "run a hot wire" around some wheat pasture. Working up different sides of the field, clipping wire to insulators, they meet at the far corner diagonally from where the pickup is parked. Elder brother says, "You got any clips in your pocket?"

"Nope."

"Go get some."

3. Elder brother and younger brother go out to check the fence. Elder is driving, and so younger gets out to scrutinize the indicator light on the fence charger.

"I think it's grounded."

Elder brother doesn't want to walk the fence. "Hold your hand over the bulb and look again."

"Oh yeah, now I think I see a little light."

Farmers and agricultural engineers paid little attention to the concept of electric fencing prior to the mid-1930s,

when the Rural Electrification Administration began assist-
ing cooperatives to electrify rural America. Before this,
some stockmen had experimented at home with batteries
hooked to coils such as those used on gasoline engines.
These little units could deliver a nasty shock, but not a dangerous one.

Centrally generated, 110-volt power brought new potential and new hazard to electric fencing. Commercial
electric fence chargers contained devices to limit and inter-
rupt the flow of current from the highline to the fence. If
these safeguards malfunctioned, or if stockmen wired
around them, electric fences could be lethal. So the hu-
morous lore of electric fences is mixed with a few horror
stories involving the deaths of humans or fine livestock.

The advantages of electric fences as economical and
flexible devices of restraint were obvious. It was only a
short leap of invention to turn the device of restraint into
an instrument of training, as many folks did—although
sometimes more for spite or mischief than for practical
effect. Placed around a mare's stall, the hot wire weaned
persistent mule colts; attached to the corners of a building,
it kept dogs away; strung through a dead chicken, sus-
pending the bird off the ground, it taught hogs not to kill
poultry.

The hot wire—such a commonplace item on the farm,
but such a curious object to reflect upon. Who knows
to what use it has been put within the reaches of the
plains?—*TI*

78. *Electric Fences*

TOM is from central Kansas, where wheat pasture and electric fencing go together like urban cowboys and Skoal. My
home was in the tall grass of the Flint Hills, where we didn't
have much wheat, but I do remember a few things about
electric fences.

We had a six-volt line that used an automobile battery for power. You could hear it thumping from a hundred feet away when the battery was strong. We didn't have little metal rod posts with clip-on insulators to hold the tiny picture-frame wire that makes up most electric-fencing units today. Instead, we used barbed wire fastened to white ceramic insulators which, in turn, were nailed to hedge posts.

While a car battery doesn't begin to carry the zap that a highline unit does, it can still wake you up, especially if the ground is a bit damp. It can also cause a saddle horse to get lively if he's being led across a wire pressed to the ground and a jolt goes through the line just about the time a horseshoe hits it.

Hot wires have been put to some interesting uses. When I was in graduate school in Missouri, we ran some steers on rented pasture. Our landlady was a strong believer in electric fences. She had them not only around the perimeter of the pastures and the soybean fields, but also two wires around her garden.

The garden wires, however, were not there to keep cattle out. Instead one wire was about three inches off the ground, the other six inches above it. She raised good sweet corn and never lost a single ear to raccoons. Not only that, but stray dogs never investigated one of her garden posts more than once.

I talked to a Texan a while back who used a hot wire to kill the rattlesnakes that abounded near his house. He would sprinkle the ground in the evening, getting it nice and damp, then plug in a bare wire that was hung just a few inches above the ground. This was not a livestock electric fence but a regular 110-volt line. In the morning he would unplug the wire and go around and pick up the dead rattlers that had crawled under the wire. They had gotten a tingle when crawling over the damp ground, then risen to strike—but electricity struck them first.

Wilbur Thompson (my father-in-law), who lives near Chanute, Kansas, installed a solar-operated electric fence

nearly two years ago. The photoelectric cells draw energy
from the sun and keep the fence, which has about the same
power as a highline model, running constantly—even at
night. In fact, according to the guarantee, it is supposed to
run for three weeks without any sunlight whatever.

Back before I was married, I learned something else
about electric fencing from Wilbur: if several people are
holding hands and one of them grabs the hot line, only the
person on the end of the line will get shocked. Over the
years the grandkids all seem to have learned that trick, one
they love to play on their city cousins.

My favorite bit of electric-fence folklore concerns the
town know-it-all who accidentally touched a hot wire one
day, his hand involuntarily jerking back when the charge
hit him. One of his fellow whittlers commented: "Got
shocked, did you Charley?" "Nope," he replied calmly, "I
was too quick for it."—*JH*

79. *Monkeys and Hot Wires*

EARLIER I mentioned some of the electric-fence lore I had
learned from my father-in-law, Wilbur Thompson, of Chanute, Kansas. Wilbur also told me another hot-wire story
that I think deserves to be recorded.

It seems that he first heard of electric fences in about
1936 when he read an advertisement in a farm magazine
about both a battery and a highline model made by the
Prime Company. The company was selling each model for
around thirty-five dollars, but they were also offering deal-
erships to enterprising farmers.

Wilbur has always been the enterprising sort, so he
wrote for details. He found out that there was a ten-dollar
markup on each model, so he got one of each for himself
at the reduced rate. He got them running and soon had
made a sale to a neighboring farmer.

But then business slowed down. He had heard, however, that Chanute was having a hard time keeping its monkeys confined to the island built for them at the city park. People were constantly complaining about monkeys in their trees, in their gardens, and poking around in their garbage cans. It was a regular nuisance, and Wilbur thought he had the answer, if he could get the city fathers to give his electric fence a try.

Somehow he got them to agree to letting him give them a demonstration. The monkey island was similar to those found in many small rural towns at that time. A water-filled moat surrounded an island containing a stone castle-like monkey house with ladders and swings of various sorts. A stone wall at the outer edge of the moat was supposed to keep the monkeys in.

Wilbur directed city workers in stringing three or four wires around the base of the moat. They connected the wires to a highline unit, then dangled a banana from one of the wires. Before long, one of the more adventuresome monkeys waded through the moat and, still standing in the water, grabbed for the banana.

The screeching and howling was heard for blocks. The money turned a backflip into the water, tore back through his astonished companions, and disappeared into the recesses of the monkey house. After a long time he was finally seen peeking out of the highest window.

The rest of the monkeys were as subdued as third-graders who have just seen the orneriest kid in class get severely reprimanded. They hightailed into the monkey house right after him and there they all stayed for hours.

Needless to say, the city officials were highly impressed. They bought the fence charger on the spot and kept it running for the next thirty years. In fact, it was still working at the time the monkey house was torn down in the late 1960s.

Wilbur retired from the electric-fence business right after that second sale. He says that he got too busy with his other farm work, but I think he realized that he could never top the excitement of the trial run at Monkey Island, so he quit while he was ahead.—*JH*

80. *The Herd Law*

WHILE we were having New Year's dinner in Great Bend, Kansas, a waitress called my brother Stan to the telephone. Said the voice on the line, "Yeah, this is the Barton County sheriff's office, and you've got cattle on the road out here." It turned out to be a little joke by a cousin calling about some matter, but those few words were enough to produce a sinking feeling in the stomach.

Ownership of stock, after all, carries responsibility and liability. That's why one of the thorniest legal questions pertaining to the settlement of the Great Plains was the herd law, a matter that raised basic issues about relations among neighbors and rights to property.

The herd law goes back to antecedents in English common law. In England owners of stock were required to restrain their animals or pay for damages to neighbors' crops. In colonial North America, this legal principle died out. Americans considered all unfenced land to be common pasture, regardless of ownership. Stock-raising entrepreneurs prospered on the open range.

The American system worked well in forested country. Farmers had to clear their croplands anyway, and so they might as well use the timber for fencing out roaming stock. Problems developed, however, when settlement reached the grasslands. Pioneer farmers protested that where timber was scarce, the cost of fencing constituted a barrier to settlement. They agitated for renewal of English common law—for a herd law.

By force of numbers, the farmers won out. In Nebraska, for instance, the legislature enacted a general herd law in 1871. The statute could be nullified only by the initiative of a majority of the voters in a particular county. Kansas's herd law, enacted in 1872, provided for county option. The county commissioners were empowered to activate the herd law or not to. Numerous local struggles over the issue ensued.

Some of the most heated conflicts involved Texans. Towns such as Abilene and Ellsworth, in Kansas, had developed as marketing points for Texas cattle on the Kansas Pacific Railway. As soon as the towns were on their feet, though, and farmers and small stockmen moved in to supply a local trade base, the commissioners of Dickinson and Ellsworth counties invoked the herd law and excluded the Texans' trade—Texans being undesirable because they encouraged vice, their cattle carried Texas fever, and they were likely to be Democrats.

Claim holders in the Flint Hills of Kansas were also upset about the inroads of transient Texas cattle and demanded a herd law in traditional small-farmer-vs.-big-capitalist rhetoric: "We want this law to protect us from the large herds that are driven in here by men who do not settle and help to improve the country, but merely turn non-residents' and railroad lands into stockyards, and allow their cattle to run at large, destroying all crops that are not strongly fortified," one wrote in 1872. "It is the interests of the many, instead of the few, that should be protected."

Only occasionally did the battle over the herd law become physical as well as legal. In 1879 a farmer in Rice County, Kansas (which had the herd law), penned up a herd of ponies belonging to two horse traders from Texas until the Texans should pay for damages done to his corn. The Texans rode through the county seat, Lyons, shooting out lamps and windows until the marshal emerged and wounded one of their mounts with a shotgun, whereupon they fled.

Still, some counties on the high plains of Texas, Oklahoma, and Kansas maintained the principle of the open range well into the twentieth century. Hamilton County,

Kansas, did not enact a herd law until 1931. "They've got us licked," one old cowman then remarked, "but it had to come."—*TI*

81. *Devil's Lanes*

MANY folklore terms include the word "devil"—dust devil (for the miniature tornadoes that pervade the plains during hot, dry spells), go-devil (for a horse-powered hay buck), devil wagon (for Henry Ford's horseless carriage), devil's box (for a fiddle); I'm sure the list could go on. Two such terms that are especially relevant to the plains experience have to do with barbed wire.

Old-timers called barbed wire the devil's hatband, a term that reveals quite clearly their disdain and disgust for the invention that signaled the end of the open range. No question about it, barbed wire is a devilish thing to work with, as anyone knows who has had hands or clothing torn by the stuff. But there is an even more visible sign of its malevolent potential—the devil's lane.

Anyone who has ever noticed a narrow lane of barbed-wire fencing, too narrow to be a road or trail, has probably seen a devil's lane. I've never stepped one off, but the ones I remember seeing looked no wider than six or eight feet. What is the purpose of such a narrow lane?

The answer is that it has no purpose; it simply stands as mute evidence of the inability of two neighbors to agree on who will care for which half of their shared fence. The name derives from the feud that precipitated the lane.

Customary practice dictates that a landowner is responsible for erecting and maintaining the half of a boundary fence that is on his right-hand side as he faces his neighbor's land. Fence law, on the other hand, dictates only that a landowner must erect and maintain half of the boundary fence—it doesn't specify which half. Fence law also dictates that if one landowner fails to maintain his half of the fence, his neighbor can build a new fence entirely on his own land, set in a few feet from the line.

Once this fence has been built, the person who had before refused to keep up the old fence is then enjoined from any use of the new fence whatsoever. That means that, if he wants to use his pasture or field for grazing, he must build a fence of his own, not set on the property line, but pulled back equally as far as that of his neighbor.

Thus the term devil's lane, because the two neighbors had acted as if inspired by the devil, not by charity and brotherly love. In addition to sustaining the ill will between neighbors, devil's lanes can have another negative side effect. A cow that somehow crawls into a devil's lane, unless the fence line crosses a running stream, can end up dying of thirst. Another example of man's inhumanity to man extending into the animal kingdom.

I don't see too many devil's lanes anymore. Maybe that's a sign that people are getting along better nowadays. Or maybe it's just that with land so dear and the agricultural economy so bad, no one can afford to give up grazing space or to build any unnecessary fence. But then virtue by necessity is better than no virtue at all.—*JH*

82. *Fence Viewers*

WRITING about herd laws, I decided that fences can separate neighbors almost as effectively as they do livestock. "Good fences make good neighbors," the adage goes. Bad ones make trouble.

A sensitive issue is the erection and maintenance of fences along the common property line of two landowners. The custom prevailed, throughout the West as far as I know, that each neighbor should keep up the half of the fence that stood on his right as he faced his neighbor's land. Sometimes, perhaps because one neighbor needed a section built before the other did, two parties might agree to abridge custom and to assume responsibility for some other part of the fence besides the right half. Poor memory or a change of ownership was likely to cause trouble later. For that matter, some folks were just bad neighbors and could not be shamed into keeping up their part of the fence.

Somehow, the law had to back up custom. In many states the legislature did this by establishing officials called "fence viewers."

I never would have known about fence viewers if I had not run across a volume labeled "Assignments of the Fence Viewers" in the office of the Register of Deeds, Greenwood County, Kansas. Checking an early version of the *General Statutes of Kansas,* I found that state law authorized the trustee, clerk, and treasurer of each township to "view fences." When neighbors had disputes about their fences, the viewers had to come to the site, examine the fence, and decide upon the obligations of the parties concerned.

Fence viewers received two dollars a day each, plus expenses, paid jointly by the parties requiring their services, or, if one of the parties was judged negligent in the dispute, by that party alone. If a fence viewer neglected his duty, he was fined two dollars and was liable for damages that might result from disrepair of the fence.

Other states had fence viewers, too. In Nebraska the law provided for committees of three fence viewers, one chosen by each of the disputants and the third chosen by the two so named. Fence viewers in Nebraska had power to subpoena witnesses and compel testimony under oath. Oklahomans chose fence viewers in the same manner as did Nebraskans. A check with law librarians at the University of Texas, though, indicates that Texas did not have fence viewers. I don't know about other states. I'd like to hear from people with experience in the matter.

The assignments I found in Greenwood County took place between 1888 and 1913. In most cases the fence viewers were called upon to require one neighbor to pay another for fence the second one had already built. The fence viewers also stipulated exactly what parts of the fence were to be maintained by what parties thereafter. Usually the fence viewers charged no expenses other than their customary two-dollar fees. An assignment in 1913, however, showed that the fence viewers hired a livery team and made the party at fault pay the hire.

These small troubles notwithstanding, the small number of entries in the record indicated that people on the plains generally worked out neighborly responsibilities among themselves and seldom resorted to the law.—*TI*

83. *Andrew Johnston's Cattle Guard*

On a hillside just east of Carroll Johnston's ranch house some twelve miles north of Watford City, North Dakota, stands a plaque commemorating the work of Andrew Johnston, Carroll's greatuncle. Johnston, the son of pioneers, was an innovator in the cattle business. He began running his own cow herd when he was barely in his teens, and early on he became a member of the South Dakota Stock Raisers' Association. Later he helped organize the first cattlemen's association in North Dakota, serving as its president at the time that it became the North Dakota Stockmen's Association. He attended over fifty meetings of the National Livestock Association and was made an honorary vice-president of that organization.

The plaque on the lonely North Dakota hillside, though, refers to none of these highlights of Andrew Johnston's life. Instead, it records his claim to an invention so lowly, so commonplace in range country, that no one else even thought of claiming it: "On this spot in 1914 Andrew Johnston invented the cattle guard."

In truth, Johnston was not the sole—not even the first—inventor of the cattle guard. Railroad cattle guards had been around since 1836, and various types of stiles (which are similar in principle to the automotive cattle guard, only intended for foot traffic) had been in use for centuries, both in this country and in Europe.

More important, at least a dozen automotive cattle guards had been built in different parts of the Great Plains before Johnston built his. T. E. Riggs and Hugh Hurley, for instance, built three in Erath County, Texas, in 1913; part of one of these is still in existence. Richard Robbins, Jr., of Pratt, Kansas, remembers seeing the date 1912 scratched into the concrete foundation of a cattle guard on the old Anchor D Ranch in the Oklahoma panhandle. Bill King, of Kim, Colorado, saw his first cattle guards near Garden City, Kansas, in 1910, while W. C. Mills, of Lake City, Kansas, knows of cattle guards built in the Gypsum Hills around 1908.

The earliest-known automotive cattle guard was built by an inventive bachelor German immigrant named Neitchez near Barr Lake, Colorado, sometime around 1905. This man built his cattle guard (of wooden poles over a pit) to accommodate his homemade automobile—which tended to die whenever it stopped moving. What happened to Neitchez, no one knows, but since 1905 his creation has been re-created hundreds of thousands of times all over the Great Plains, the nation, and the world.

But to get back to Andrew Johnston. I visited the site of his invention a few years back, and I talked with some of his many friends and relatives. He was, I determined, not only an innovator, but an honest and honorable man. He did, I am convinced, indeed invent a cattle guard just north of Watford City in 1914. It just didn't happen to have been the first, or the only, one ever invented.

The cattle guard was a device whose time had come, and in true folk fashion it was simultaneously and spontaneously created to fill the need caused by the meeting of barbed-wire fences and the automobile in the range country of the Great Plains. Still, Andrew Johnston deserves his plaque. He was, after all, the only man with enough foresight to realize the significance of what he had done and thus to have laid claim to an invention that has since become a symbol of the modern range.—*JH*

84. *Painted-Stripe Cattle Guards*

NOT LONG AGO a reader sent me a photograph of the most unusual cattle guard he had ever seen—one made of nothing but stripes of paint. Now a cattle guard, as any good plains dweller knows, is a kind of automatic gate, a pit in the road covered with parallel bars that cars can drive over but cows shy away from. Most pits are a foot or so deep, and the bars of most cattle guards are made of pipe or railroad rail—solid but rough to drive over.

In fact, one thing I learned a couple of years back when I was researching a book on the history and lore of cattle guards is that most people don't notice them at all. They don't, that is, unless they are bouncing across one that is rough enough to send shudders up their arms and throw the wheels out of alignment.

But even people who don't notice ordinary cattle guards are intrigued by the painted-stripe ones. Dozens of people wrote to tell me about them, puzzled as to how they could possibly turn cows. The scientific answer is that bovine vision lacks the sort of depth perception that can distinguish between the shadow of a real pit and the dark asphalt between the stripes of paint.

The practical answer, as any cowboy knows, is that cattle don't particularly like the hard surface of asphalt and they especially don't like no-passing stripes painted on it. It seems as if there is at least one animal in every herd that won't cross a solid line; you have to let it go down the road past the end of the yellow line and then drive it across the dark pavement between the broken white lines.

Several people have told me that they hit the brakes the first time they ever saw a painted-stripe cattle guard, slowing down and bracing themselves for bumps that never came. A few years ago John Nichols wrote a novel, *The Milagro Beanfield War*, set in rural New Mexico. One of the main characters, Sheriff Bernabe Montoya, never does get used to the painted stripes, flinching each time he drives across them. He likens them to other of society's artificial substitutes—burglar alarm signs displayed by people too cheap to install a real system, for one thing, padded bras for another.

As far as I know, no painted-stripe cattle guards are currently extant in any of the eastern tier of plains states— Texas to North Dakota. But in all the other western states they are widely used. They are also used in South Africa. The earliest one, according to oral sources, was in West Texas or eastern New Mexico as early as 1929, while the earliest documented use is in Oregon and Nevada during the first part of the 1940s.

A typical painted-stripe guard is comprised of around ten stripes, each about four inches wide and spaced about six inches apart. The first cost is relatively cheap, but even moderate traffic means a lot of repainting. Some states will alternate colors—white for one painting, yellow for the next. Others have tried variations—stripes that come to an arrow point, thus heading the animal away from the fence opening—to make them work better.

But work they do, especially with wilder cattle in thinly populated ranges. Except, I think, when it snows.—*JH*

85. *Lawsuits, Hedgehogs, and Cattle Guards*

ONE of the most troublesome decisions faced by those of us who like to research and write is knowing when to quit researching and start writing. Not only is researching usually fun and writing often painful, but one also runs the risk of missing some interesting details by rushing into print.

In late 1982, for instance, I published *The Cattle Guard* with the University Press of Kansas, having spent some five years tracking down every reference to cattle guards I could uncover. Sure enough, shortly after it had gone to press, a couple of things happened that I wish I could have gotten into the book.

One was my short-lived career as an expert witness. A

lawyer representing the State Highway Department of New Mexico called in June, 1982, wanting some advice in a lawsuit. It seems that a few months earlier a motorist had hit a cow in the middle of the night, and both the rancher and the state were being sued for not maintaining the cattle guard where the cow had escaped the pasture.

I was flown to Albuquerque, put up in a nice hotel there, then flown by the attorney, in his company's twin-engine plane, on to Alamogordo the next morning. There we rented a car and drove to Tula Rosa where I did some measuring and photographing.

I wasn't sure how effective my testimony would be for the Highway Department, because I thought that this particular cattle guard was neither installed carefully nor well maintained. Still, I got a call the next week telling me to catch a plane out of Wichita and come on down for the trial. Fortunately for my nerves, I got another call shortly after the first one telling me that they had settled out of court.

The second item was more unusual, even appearing in the *New Yorker* as one of their "There'll always be an England" fillers at the end of a column, although I had heard of it a couple of months earlier—but too late to include in the book.

It seems that a retired English army major, Adrian Coles, of Ludlow, discovered a hedgehog trapped inside what the British call a cattle grid. "I realized that cattle grids are death traps as far as hedgehogs are concerned," said Major Coles, so he started the British Hedgehog Preservation Society. One of their major functions is to see that an escape ramp is installed in every cattle guard in the British Isles.

According to Coles, the escape ramp works like a charm. The little creatures wander around in the pit until they run across the ramp, then up and out they go.

We don't have hedgehogs in this country, but we do have plenty of other small animals that could fall between the bars of a cattle guard. Still the pits here are not much of a problem because most American cattle guards are open on one or both ends. Even the pits that are enclosed are usually shallow enough for a rabbit or an opossum to hop or crawl out of.

The one critter that would seem to benefit most from an escape ramp in our cattle guards is the box tortoise. Still, in all of the hundreds of cattle guards that I examined while doing my research, I never saw a turtle in one. The biggest threat to their safety seems to be the careless motorist, not the cattle guard.—*JH*

Part Eight

PEOPLE AND PLACES

Now that the white around my knuckles has given way to a more natural coloration and I can again straighten my fingers into something other than a death-grip-on-the-steering-wheel shape, I think I will compare the attractions of the Great Plains with those of the mountains.

This urge to praise the flatlands results from a recent visit to the Rockies and some tent camping at nine thousand feet, about twenty-five miles south of Telluride, Colorado. It seems as if every couple of years or so I am drawn into the mountains so that I can appreciate the plains even more than I usually do.

Now, I like the mountains. I am not at all drawn into them in the same way that I am drawn into the reptile house at a zoo. I go for pleasure, not safely to view something that normally repels me. I like the camping, the fresh air, the clear streams, and the trout fishing. But I can take only so much before I begin to feel claustrophobic, to feel overpowered by the towering trees and rocks.

The worst part, though, is the driving. I'm not as bad as the Oklahoma driver who preceded me on one stretch of the Million Dollar Highway joining Silverton and Ouray, Colorado, a flatlander who slowed literally to a stop on every switchback curve, but I do drive much more slowly (and cautiously and fearfully—and safely) than do the Coloradans and the Texans. They even pull camping trailers behind four-horse trailers behind their four-wheel-drive pickups!

On the way out we crossed Wolf Creek Pass, made famous a few years back by a country song about a trucker who loses his brakes and ends up scattering chicken feathers all over Pagosa Springs (the lyrics refer to "hairpin curves and switchback city" and road maps that "look like a malaria germ"). Believe me, Wolf Creek Pass is like a run between Amarillo and Lubbock, Texas, compared to Molas

Pass between Durango and Silverton. Even worse is Red Mountain Pass that must be crossed to get from Silverton to Ouray.

Worst of all was Bolam Pass, a dirt road that led twenty miles east from our campsite to Purgatory, just north of Durango. It is marked on the forest-service maps as a four-wheel-drive road, and it is narrow and steep. Just as we were getting to the end (maybe four miles to go) and my hands were beginning to relax on the steering wheel, the brakes went crazy—my foot going clear to the floor when I pressed them, but otherwise sticking so that when I drove, the engine was fighting both gravity and the brakes. Fortunately, we made it to the highway and a couple of miles on into Needles, Colorado, where a garageman, as nice as any I have found on the plains, fixed the brakes, and for a reasonable price.

But to get back to the relative attractions of the mountains and the plains—no question that the mountains are spectacularly beautiful, that they call forth spontaneous oohs and aahs, but they are essentially barren. Relatively few cattle or sheep can be pastured there. Crops will grow only in the valleys, only for a short season, and only with plenty of irrigation. Most of the trout are there because the Fish and Game workers raise replacements by the thousands to keep the streams and lakes stocked. You can't even drink from the crystal-clear streams because they are infested with a dangerous parasite.

About the only wealth in the mountains (not counting the tourist dollars—or, to be fair, timber) comes from mining. Fabulous riches have been found inside those beautiful peaks, but the mountains are not beautiful once the miners have finished with them. Entire mountains are sometimes gobbled up and run through machines that spit out gravel and sludge while extracting the ore. Large lakes of sterile, stagnant refuse and fishless rivers running with cloudy, yellowish water lie below the piles of slag.

The plains, on the other hand, can be (and are) used

over and over without diminishing their beauty. Provided, that is, that one sees beauty in grasslands, milo fields, or wheat stubble. I do. In fact, I think that Colorado Highway 10 between La Junta and Walsenburg just might be the prettiest drive in the state.

The plains may be plain, but at least their productivity is not limited to a one-time ravaging. Properly nurtured, the farms and ranches of the Great Plains year after year produce an economic abundance that far outstrips the fabled riches of any of the legendary motherlodes of the mountains.—*JH*

87. *On the Sod-House Frontier*

T. LINDSAY BAKER spent the winters of '79–80 and '80–81 in a sod house. If that doesn't strike you as unusual, let me explain. I'm talking about 1979–80 and 1980–81, not 1879–80 and 1880–81.

As mentioned earlier, Lindsay works for the Panhandle-Plains Historical Museum, in Canyon, Texas. With the help of volunteers he built a sod house, near Canyon, on the Nance Ranch, owned by West Texas State University. The soddy was to be the site of interpretive programs about life on the sod-house frontier.

Lindsay and his co-workers cut sod with a grasshopper plow from the museum collection (drawn by a John Deere tractor, however), cut it into blocks with spades, and hauled the blocks to the building site in a pickup. They marked out the dimensions with twine and laid up the walls, 2½ feet thick at the bottom and tapered to 2 feet, each block tamped down with a maul. The house measured 24 feet by 18 feet outside. The ceiling was 7½ feet. The doors and windows were framed with used lumber.

The roof had a ridgepole under the gable, rafters parallel to the ridgepole, and one-inch lumber and tar paper laid across the rafters. Cedar posts, set at the corners, kept cattle from rubbing the walls down. About the place was strewn "appropriate trash," such as old kerosene cans.

"In building a sod house, you really learn to appreciate the fellows who built the ones in historical photographs," Lindsay says. "Those guys were good."

It would have been easy for Lindsay to dress up in his overalls, work boots, collarless shirt, and felt hat and go out to the sod house whenever the museum had visitors scheduled. Instead he chose to live there. He slept on an iron bed with a cotton mattress, cooked on a Sears-Roebuck stove, heated with an Estate caboose stove, and swept a dirt floor. One concession to gentility: for bathing, he took a swim each day at the university pool.

Cats reduced the number of mice and, presumably, made the place less attractive to snakes. "Presumably," I say, because Lindsay killed eleven rattlesnakes the first year and six the next, nailing the severed rattles above the door.

For visitors, mostly school kids, Lindsay assumed the role of a cotton farmer from East Texas, displaced by hard times and boll weevils, who had come to West Texas to get rich. Someday, he told them, he would replace the soddy with a big, white, frame house. Meanwhile, he farmed as best he could, did windmill work on the side, lived in fear of illness or injury, and got lonely. He sure was happy to see them. And he sure was interested in the odd things they had in their lunch pails ("What is this 'Dr. Pepper'? Do you have consumption?").

Lindsay showed his guests how to soften harness with bacon fat, wash clothes on a board, and do other chores common to the Great Plains frontier. Bad boys and girls he sent out with a wheelbarrow to gather cow chips.

Eventually, Lindsay decided to get married and moved out of the sod house. It hadn't been a bad experience, though, he says. "Ninety-five percent of the nights I went to sleep with the sound of the coyotes singing."—*TI*

88. *Oil-field Camps*

FOR three generations now, ever since we Americans awoke
to the realization that ours was no longer a nation with a
frontier, we have looked back and mourned the days when
sturdy, bold, individualistic pioneers could escape the con-
straints of society and make a new start somewhere in the
golden West. The more I study the proposition, though,
the more I doubt the importance of the fiddle-footed fron-
tiersman on the Great Plains. To me it seems that the culture of our region is much more the product of ordinary
people seeking satisfactory community life. I am sure that
my ancestors sought here not anarchy but rather the opportunity to be part of a developing, new community.

The same was true of other people on the plains, even
under the most difficult conditions. For instance, consider
the residents of hundreds of oil-field company camps that
sprang up during the rapid plays in various parts of the
plains. Moved about by whim of the company, these people
still sought to re-create the sort of community and family
life that they had grown up with and considered proper.

An acquaintance of mine, Grace Dobler, of Madison,
Kansas, has talked to numerous oil-field camp residents
about this, among them George and Doris McGhee, of
Madison. During the 1920s and 1930s, the McGhees lived
on a Superior (later Sun-Ray) Oil lease near St. Louis community, Greenwood County.

Churches and schools were rallying points for oil-field
communities. For the McGhees these were the Prairie
Chapel, in St. Louis, and the St. Louis School. "The school
was the big social point of our lives," said Doris. There was
some kind of program every month: a musical program, a
play, a box supper, an ice-cream social, or a card party
(from which the McGhees had to abstain because of religious scruples).

It was important that there be a strong, independent
feminine society in the camps, because the men were away

working twelve-hour shifts ("We'd swing a lantern in the morning and one at night," remarked George). Women of the camp sat with one another's sick children (there were always sick children in an oil-field camp), formed afternoon clubs, and got together for sewing. The only cool place for the group to sew during summer was the cave, or storm cellar.

Many social gatherings centered around music. In the St. Louis area were two accordians, a piano, a guitar, and a violin. People dropped in for group singing, and Doris gave piano lessons for thirty-five cents a lesson. "We had lots of social life around the lease, especially in winter," she summed up.

The basic unit of community, the family, also remained strong. The McGhees were married in 1924 (and were to live in company houses until 1954). Formerly a roustabout, George, as a married man, settled into a pumper's job. The job was a permeating influence on family life. "You had to keep those wells running," George said, "and if you didn't, somebody was there to take your place." Doris, meanwhile, drew hot water to wash his greasy clothes from the circulating tank at the powerhouse.

Annual flowers and annual coats of paint helped make presentable the company houses, constructed of wide siding with no wallboarding inside. "And we'd wallpaper, and we'd paint, and we tried so hard to fix those houses up so they'd look like a home"—how easily those words of Doris McGhee, oil-field wife, might have been those of a calvaryman's bride in a lonely outpost, or a pioneer farmwife in a sodhouse, or many another homemaker on the plains.—*TI*

89. *In Saskatchewan*

A MID-WINTER lecture and research tour in Saskatchewan started me to thinking about the similarities and differences between life in the prairie provinces of Canada and in the southern plains of the United States. These two areas, since they are the extremities of the same general region, the North American Great Plains, do have many things in common. They are generally flat, treeless, and subhumid to semiarid, and these conditions shape similar customs and institutions in various parts of the plains.

Still, generally speaking, the economy of both the American and the Canadian plains is based on small grains (mostly wheat) to an extent in some places approaching monoculture. I had thought that in my travels over the winter wheatlands of Kansas, Texas, Oklahoma, and Colorado, I had seen oceans of amber waves, but nowhere had I seen such uninterrupted tracts of wheat ground as I saw in Saskatchewan.

I thought about that as I rode from Regina, capital of Saskatchewan, to the village of Briarcrest, just southeast of Moose Jaw. Jack Boan, an economist at the University of Regina, drove me to Briarcrest to talk with his father, Alexander, and his mother, Dorothy, about their experiences farming in the area.

Two particular differences between the economic situation there and that of the southern plains seemed to me to be products of our different political and social systems. The first was that Briarcrest, like many comparable villages up there, had a cooperative general store. Organizations such as the Grange and the Farmer's Alliance tried cooperative stores in the states of the southern plains during the nineteenth century, but they died out rather rapidly, and since then co-ops here largely have been confined to agribusiness operations. Not so in Saskatchewan, which retains a strong tradition of cooperation, and for that matter, at the provincial level, what we in the states would consider outright socialism.

The second difference I noticed was that farmers in Saskatchewan store much more of their grain on the farm than we do on the southern plains. On every farmstead stood a cluster of wood-frame granaries. Grain elevators along the railroad, on the other hand, had little or no storage capacity. I think this difference is tied to the operation in Canada of the government wheat pool.

To get back to the Boans—I visited with them about their earliest recollections of farming methods. Since settlement of their locality was about two decades later than settlement of most of the southern plains, their memories stretched back to the beginnings of agriculture in the area. They remembered technological developments that occurred before the time of most living residents of the southern plains.

Alexander Boan is ninety-five years old, and as a boy he bucked straw from a horsepower threshing outfit. This rig was driven by six teams walking in a circle to turn a horsepower sweep connected by a tumbling rod to the separator. Boan later did custom threshing with his own steam outfit. How many plainsmen living today can say that they witnessed the transition from horsepower threshing to steam?

And how many ever saw a reaper in operation? Binders and headers, yes, but Alexander Boan hand-tied bundles behind a self-rake reaper. If he hadn't been laid up with a bad leg, I would have gotten him outside to show me how to twist a straw band and hand-tie a bundle of wheat.—*TI*

90. *At the Stann Farm*

AFTER visiting with the Boans of Briarcrest, I met another Saskatchewan farm family, the Stanns, of Southey, near Markinch. Emil Jonescu, of Regina, took me to their place so that I could see a good-sized wheat-and-cattle operation. Reaching the farm by a drive through the Qu' Appelle valley, I learned how many disadvantages farmers in the prairie provinces of Canada struggle against in order to compete with their counterparts on the southern plains of the United States.

As we drove across the Stann place, I remarked to Emil

how rocky and light the soil appeared. On arriving at the farmstead, though, I knew immediately that the Stanns were enterprising folk, capable of dealing with their harsh surroundings. Around their house stood stately shelterbelts of blue spruce trees. I had become dismayed about the absence of wildlife in the countryside—not so much as a field sparrow to be seen in hours of driving—but as I approached the Stann house, the music of a hundred songbirds greeted me.

The oldest member of the household was Constantine Stann, a native of Rumania, who arrived in Canada with the name Stanciulescu. Because of later settlement of the Canadian prairie provinces, they are populated with many more eastern Europeans than are the American southern plains, where western Europeans (Germans, Scandinavians, and other blond-haired folk) predominate.

Constantine Stann's great agricultural interest is sheep, and I would have liked to have talked to him about it, but unfortunately, I don't speak Rumanian. So while he and Emil conversed in their native tongue, I posed all sorts of questions to John (Constantine's son) and Mary, his wife.

The Stanns raise registered Herefords. In past decades, while Hereford breeders in the states developed short, compact animals, the Stanns continued to produce rangier stock. In recent years they have begun to exhibit at the Denver stock show, and they have done extremely well, because they brought their lankier animals down just when stockmen's preferences were returning to their kind of animal.

As John Stann observes, though, their stock raising takes place in economic isolation. There is in Saskatchewan no such substantial cattle-finishing industry as exists on the southern plains. The feed grains that foster cattle feeding on the southern plains have no equivalent substitutes in Canada. The dearth of feed grains, it seems to me, is the major obstacle preventing the healthy diversification of farming in the prairie provinces.

Single-cropping of wheat in a simple wheat-fallow rotation has led to some peculiar problems. On fallow ground, alkali water rises to the surface, saturating the soil with minerals and creating a hard crust. Soil specialists urge farmers to continuous-crop their wheat to prevent alkali buildup, but farmers insist on summer fallowing to accumulate moisture.

I was happy to hear John Stann tell how he solved the problem on their place, because his solution was typically eastern European. He just covered his alkali patches with all the manure he could get his hands on.

Unfortunately, few of Stann's neighbors had manure to cover their alkali spots. I told him that I would be happy to set up a deal whereby feedlot operators in southwest Kansas or northwest Texas could supply the Canadians with all the manure they wanted. He said that he would let me know when they needed it, but he hasn't called yet.—*TI*

91.   *POWs on the Plains*

How PEACEFUL it must have seemed to soldiers of Erwin Rommel's Afrika Korps when they found themselves in the farmlands of the American plains. Thousands of German prisoners of war spent the latter years of World War II in internment camps here, producing numerous interesting encounters between Americans and the alleged "Nazis."

It made good sense to send German POWs to camps in the plains states, rather than interning them in Africa and Europe, where they were captured. Vessels carrying American troops to the European theater might as well carry along German prisoners as sail back empty; the presence of the German prisoners might even afford some measure of security from submarine attack. It was easier to supply camps in the United States than in Europe. Prisoners had little chance to escape from the heartland of the United States. And perhaps most important, in accordance with the Geneva Convention, prisoners of war could be deployed as laborers in factories and on farms.

On the plains, POWs worked mainly for farmers. At base camps, such as those near Concordia and Salina, Kansas, or at branch camps, such as those in Peabody, Hays, Council Grove, Hutchinson, El Dorado, Eskridge, and dozens of other locations, farmers could pick up prisoners, usually in groups of four, to work for them. For this labor the farmers paid low-to-prevailing wages, of which the prisoners themselves received a part.

Between the farmers and the prisoners there developed working relationships and sometimes even cordial friendships. For instance, the Peabody, Kansas, camp was located in the heart of the German-Russian Mennonite area of the state. Most residents of the area were fluent in German and could converse readily with the POWs.

Like other local farmers, Ernest Claassen, whom I interviewed for a television show at his farm near Peabody, picked up prisoner laborers at the Eyestone Building, where they were quartered (this building, bars on the windows, still stands and now houses a manufacturing firm). The men performed a variety of tasks for him; hauling manure was one of the big jobs.

The greatest labor need in the locality, though, was for men to assist in threshing kaffir corn and other grain sorghums. The kaffir was cut with a corn binder, shocked, and finally threshed out with a combine. The five-foot Allis-Chalmers combine was designed so that the sickle could be tilted up. The prisoners not only shocked the kaffir but also took the bundles from the shocks and laid the heads on the combine's upturned sickle to be cut off and threshed.

Kansas was hot, and kaffir was itchy, much to the laborers' discomfort. One of them even made up a rhyme about it. "Gott schuf Menschen, Affen, Tiere," he said, "und in seinem grossen Zorn, schuf er Kansas und das Kaffir Corn" ("God created the men, apes, and other animals, and then in his great wrath, created Kansas and kaffir corn").

Yet hard work and contact with families stimulated good relations between POWs and local residents. Christina Claassen, Ernest's wife, still recalls the grateful, incredulous expressions on the faces of the German prisoners the first time she called them in German for dinner at her table. Thousands of miles removed from their homes and their military obligations, the men seemed more forlorn than fierce.—*TI*

92. *Hidden Places*

A FEW YEARS AGO, I worked with the Kansas Committee for the Humanities in preparing a traveling program called "Hidden Places." The program consisted of three films, to be presented with commentary, of little-known places of significant historical interest: sites in Kansas and Wyoming along the Oregon Trail, mining ghost towns in Idaho and Montana, and Indian petroglyphs in West Texas.

More recently, the KCH has sponsored a series of eight radio programs dealing specifically with "hidden places" in Kansas. The programs are well researched and concern such things as the Cimarron National Grassland in Morton County, the Chanute Mexican Fiesta, the Brown Opera House in Concordia, Dr. Hertzler's house near Halstead, and an Indian-made prehistoric stone man near Hill City.

All this work has made me realize that the entire plains region is full of hidden places. Many of these sites have a legendary aura about them. Near my hometown, for instance, is a place called Dead Man's Hollow. According to a local story that has survived nearly a hundred years, two men and a woman were passing through in a covered wagon. One man, the husband, left the camp, knocked on a nearby farmer's door, and asked to be taken in, saying that he was afraid. For whatever reason, his request was denied and the next day the wagon moved on to the southwest and was never seen again. A few weeks later, however, the farmer was out hunting and the barking of his dogs attracted him to a couple of tall cottonwood trees. There, in a shallow grave, he found the body of the husband, murdered by his wife and her lover.

The two cottonwoods, from that time on, cast eerie shadows, and later, when they died, one tree fell into the arms of the other, remaining that way until the years caused their final decay.

Another legendary location is in Linn County, Kansas—Guthrie's Mound. According to a story told me recently, sometime near the end of the last century a schoolteacher named Guthrie was accosted by a mob of vigilantes. They accused him of horse stealing, refusing to believe him when he said that he had recently bought the horse from a man he thought was a horse trader. As they were lynching him, he placed a curse upon them that would deny them natural deaths. And, according to local tradition, every single member of the mob did indeed die violently.

Almost every bit of high ground near an old trail is traditionally the lookout site of either Indian or outlaw raiders. Some of these locations, such as Pawnee Rock along the Santa Fe Trail, are well-known and well-marked. Others have more local fame. Many, such as one point on the eastern part of the Santa Fe Trail near present Harveyville, are called Robbers' Roost. Here, I was told by a longtime resident of Eskridge, Kansas, outlaws would scout approaching wagon trains, passing over large, well-protected ones and preying on weaker game. The outlaw gang was finally wiped out by soldiers, and I am told that the hangings took place on a large tree that at one time grew out at an angle from the bluff.

There are, from Texas to Canada, literally scores of other such interesting local landmarks, hidden places filled with hidden history.—*JH*

93. *Butcher Shops*

To one who takes pride in his own region, the saddest
effect of the modern American food industry is the stan-
dardization of tastes it imposes. Consumers who swill low-
fat milk, pop their biscuits out of a can, and reach com-
pulsively for nationally advertised foodstuffs may enjoy a
certain security in expectations, but they never know the
adventure that comes from sampling the diversity of regional foods.

It's time that we recognize, patronize, and preserve the
small businesses of the plains that offer us foods characteristic of our region's peoples and communities. That's why,
whenever possible, I buy meat products from little butcher
shops and lockers that still do things their own way.

I visited with George Brant, who with his son, Doug,
owns and operates Brant's Market of Lucas, Kansas (the
same town where S. P. Dinsmoor's extravaganza in concrete, the Garden of Eden, is located). This red-tile, brick-
faced establishment is famous for Brant's bologna, a fine
beef product. The Brants note on their business card
that Lucas is "The only place in the world where you can
buy Brant's homemade bologna and view the Garden of
Eden."

George Brant's father, James, a Czech immigrant, came
to Wilson, Kansas, in 1911. He bought the market in Lucas
in 1922. As the business developed, its products and services reflected both the requirements of the community
and the ethnic origins of the Brants. They did general
butchering, made bologna for the general public market,
and produced several ethnic specialties—*jaternice* (liver
sausage), headcheese, blood sausage, and so on. This was
hardly the stuff that the modern consumer finds under cellophane in the supermarket.

Another good example of a local market is the Burdick
Locker, operated by Gary and Marilyn Hageberg, in Burdick, Kansas. Burdick was a Swedish settlement. Gary's fa-

ther, Olaf, a Swedish immigrant, started his meat business in 1921.

Here again the proprietors did general butchering, developed some house specialties, and perpetuated immigrant food traditions. Although Gary Hageberg says most of the "old-time Swedes" are gone now, he still makes potato sausage and imports *lutfisk* (dried fish) to cater to those with traditional tastes.

Most outsiders who visit the white-frame Burdick Locker ("Your meat's best friend," the sign says) come for the dried beef, a delicacy that has won the Hagebergs many awards from the state meat-processors' association.

The Great Plains will be culturally diminished if businesses such as Brant's Market and the Burdick Locker disappear. Federal regulations force them to curtail operations—the Brants no longer make blood sausage—while the pervading influence of the national media undermines the appeal of local producers. If they are to hold out, the next generation of proprietors will have to be just as stubborn as their immigrant forebears.—*TI*

94. *The Big Salt Plain*

LOOK at the place-names on a map—Salina, Kansas; Salina, Oklahoma; Boone's Lick, Missouri—and it's plain what an important natural resource salt was to early settlers. Sources of salt, just as they were gathering places for animals seeking the substance, became focal points also for regional history. Such a place was the Big Salt Plain of Oklahoma.

I refer here not to the Great Salt Plains near Cherokee, but to the little-known Big Salt Plain located where Buffalo Creek joins the Cimarron River, just west of the little town of Freedom. I am both intrigued by the strange history of the place and awed by its stark lonesomeness each time I visit it.

The Big Salt Plain is about five thousand acres of red sand. Groundwater impregnated with salt from underground deposits seeps to the surface and evaporates to leave a shimmering crust. In some places, brine springs flow freely, forming, through evaporation, thick beds of square salt crystals. Along the southern perimeter of the salt plain rises a rugged escarpment of red shale capped by white gypsum.

Osage, Pawnee, and Comanche Indians visited the place to obtain salt, capture horses, kill buffalo, and make war on one another. Various white explorers, including George C. Sibley, in 1811, and Nathan Boone (son of Daniel Boone), in 1843, came to the salt plain and carried away salt crystals. But the strangest tale about the site is the story of the salt mountain.

The Osages annually came to the Big Salt Plain to procure salt, and they referred to it as their "salt mountain" because they gathered salt at the foot of a cliff. That concept was difficult to translate to Spanish and French officials of Louisiana, however; the idea inevitably came out as "montaña de sal," literally a mountain of salt. So when President Thomas Jefferson, in 1803, bought the great pig-in-a-poke, Louisiana, from France, one of the things he expected to lie within it was a mountain of salt. Thus he informed a special session of Congress, and his political enemies had wonderful sport poking fun at the naïve Republican president who believed in a salt mountain.

All of this was of little concern to later settlers of southern Kansas and the Cherokee Outlet of Oklahoma who came to the Big Salt Plain to get stock salt. Since the stuff was soggy as it lay on the ground, they piled it with pitchforks into waist-high piles they called "doodles," later loading it into wagons to haul home. Efforts of local speculators to form mining companies and exploit the saline resources of the place more fully came to naught.

That is, until the arrival of an upstart named Ezra Blackmon. I've spent a couple of days with him, and although he's suspicious of people asking him questions, he's so naturally talkative that he couldn't help spilling quite a bit of his personal history. He started hauling salt from the Big Salt Plain with mules and wagons in 1920. Through a variety of legal devices he eventually won control of the entire plain. He introduced more sophisticated machinery, expanded markets for salt, went broke once, regained his holdings, and finally won a contract supplying the Oklahoma Highway Department with salt to spread on roads.

I'll never forget the look on old Ezra's face when he wondered aloud what would become of his salt plain when he and Alta were gone and whether some worthy young man would take the place of the son he lacked.—*TI*

95. *Plains Place-Names*

A MAJOR CONCERN of folklore studies is place-names. What people call a town, for instance, can be very informative. My theory is that Great Plains denizens have an introverted pride about where they live. We think that only the tough ones (like us) can make it out here, but we can also be a little defensive about having chosen to remain in such an apparently drab, difficult environment.

How is all this reflected in place-names? Well, as a little experiment (not overly-scientific) I went through my Rand-McNally road atlas and discovered sixty-seven towns in twenty-seven states and four provinces with some form of "plain" or "plains" in their titles. Only fifteen of the United States towns, however, are in the plains states, and even then only half (Texas, Kansas, Nebraska, South Dakota, and Montana) are represented. There are only four Canadian "plains" towns—one each in Quebec, Manitoba, Saskatchewan, and Alberta. "Prairie," on the other hand, appears in twenty-two town names in twelve states and two provinces. Of these towns, seventeen are located in what is considered the prairie region of the Midwest.

It would seem from these statistics that "prairie" is

thought to be a more positive term by local inhabitants than is "plain." Also, a flat grassy area would stand out as a landmark of sorts in a forested, hilly region, which might account for the numerous "plains" town names in the eastern United States.

In the plains states and provinces themselves, Texas leads the list of plains- or prairie-named towns: Grand Prairie, Prairie View, Plains, Plainview, South Plains, and Cross Plains. Texas also has some plains towns with Spanish names: Pampa, Plano, and Llano. Kansas comes in next with six such names: Prairie Village, Pretty Prairie, Plains, Plainville, Garden Plain, and Belle Plaine. South Dakota has a Plainview and a Prairie City; Montana, a town called Plains; and Nebraska, a Plainview. Alberta has a Stony Plain; Saskatchewan, a Porcupine Plain; and Manitoba, a Gilbert Plains.

Other than that, residents of the plains have avoided naming their towns anything that might suggest flatness—except Texas, which has a Levelland (way out in the Panhandle) and a Flatonia (which may or may not have anything to do with flatness).

Often early developers on the plains gave names to their towns that suggested lushness and fertility (names that might have gotten them in trouble if there had been truth-in-advertising laws back then): Garden City (Kansas), Belfield (North Dakota), Grainfield (Kansas), Wheatland (Wyoming), Bloomfield (Montana).

Plainfield is the most common single "plains" town name, occurring in fifteen states (not one of them west of Iowa). There are ten Plainviews (three in plains states) and seven Plainvilles (only one west of the Mississippi).

While a town such as Plain Dealing, Louisiana, obviously did not get its name from the surrounding terrain, most of the "plains" towns, I am sure, did. Consider the case of Plainview, Texas. Local tradition, according to Doug McDonaugh, has it that a cowboy borrowed a buckboard one Sunday afternoon in order to take his girlfriend on a picnic. The young couple drove for miles looking for a secluded spot, but every time they looked back they could still see her parents rocking back and forth on the front porch. There wasn't even a tree or boulder to hide behind.

Finally the cowboy turned the buggy around and headed back with these words to his girl, "We might as well go back. No matter how hard we try, we're still in plain view."—*JH*

96. *The Allure of the Plains*

To MANY PEOPLE the distinctive feature of the Great Plains is the seeming lack of distinctive features—the apparent plainness that gives the region its name. Outsiders who travel across the plains constantly complain about the flatness and monotony, while plains dwellers either suffer in silence or subconsciously suppress the monotony.

To the true plainsman, however, the plains are not featureless, and they are certainly not monotonous. Monotony, like beauty, is in the eye of the beholder. I found that out the summer of 1983, when our family took a three-week trip to the Pacific Northwest. There's no question about the beauty of that area—the Cascade Mountains, the Columbia River, Vancouver Island, the Inside Passage.

But I have to admit that as we started the long trip back, driving east from Anacortes, Washington, through Bismark, North Dakota, then south to Kansas, I was genuinely happy when we hit central Montana and the evergreen-covered mountains began to give way to grass-covered hills. It's not that I didn't like the scenery in the Far West—I did; but mountains make me a little uneasy. I like to visit them, but I wouldn't want to live there. I'm like one of Ace Reid's cartoon cowpokes who, sitting on a ramshackle porch and looking out across miles and miles of West Texas, said, "They ought to make this a national park. There aren't any trees or mountains to get in the way of the view."

I've talked to people who moved from the mountains to

the plains, and they invariably say that they miss them. They feel vulnerable, almost naked, without the comfort of being surrounded by the rocks and trees of high country, without being able to look up and see the looming shadow of mountains. My feeling is just the opposite. I feel vulnerable in the mountains, and claustrophobic. Who knows what's hiding behind those rocks? Who knows when some sheer, rock-covered, tree-crowned slope is going to turn loose and become a landslide? The long, seemingly endless roads of the plains are dangerous to drive only if you get drowsy; there are no two-thousand-foot precipices to fall from.

Plains folk take space and openness for granted. It seems that most of the things we think of as typical of the plains—barbed-wire fences, windmills, wheat fields, grass—are things we can see through. In fact, if we can't see through something (whether a physical object or somebody's scheme), we get nervous. Most people from outside the plains, if they seek privacy when they are out-of-doors, will look for a tree or a big rock to hide behind. Most plainsmen, on the other hand, will look for the barest, highest spot they can find. That way they can see whether or not anyone is sneaking up on them.

Coronado, we are told, was never more frightened than when he looked through the legs of a bison and could see nothing but horizon. The plains must have looked as endless to him as Interstate 70 does to a westbound easterner—four lanes into eternity. Buffalo Bill Cody, on the other hand, thought the plains anything but monotonous. He never got lost, he said, because the plains were so beautiful that every landscape he ever saw was forever emblazoned into his memory.

Mountains and trees have their attractions, but to a true plainsmen, nothing is prettier, or more reassuring, than a big sky and some wide-open spaces.—*JH*

Index of Names